"Bernie Van De Walle presents a readable, engaging, and theologically sound conversation that is absolutely necessary. Approaching a subject that has fallen out of popularity within the contemporary Christian church, Van De Walle offers a much-needed corrective to the misrepresentations of holiness that have arisen over the past several decades. By connecting the lines between God's nature and God's intention for creation, Van De Walle invites us to embrace the genuine liberty to participate in the divine nature and to be conformed to the image of Christ. He reminds us that holiness is neither something we achieve nor a matter of behavior—of being sinless—but is rather something God creates within individuals and the church. For pastors and theological educators who have lamented the current state of holiness among our parishioners and students, *Rethinking Holiness* provides an excellent resource for reigniting conversations about genuine holiness with those to whom we are called to minister."

—**Estrelda Alexander**, William Seymour College

"Van De Walle has pulled off a small miracle: he has written a book of theology that's also a page-turner. He has a gift for rendering complex ideas in lively prose with lucid arguments—and presenting it all as nourishment for the soul. In *Rethinking Holiness* he employs this gift on a topic the church urgently needs to rediscover: holiness. I am going to recommend this book widely in the hope that it reintroduces to the church (and to the world) the staggering beauty of God's holiness and invites us again to delight in the good news that God shares God's own holiness with us in order to makes us holy as God is holy."

—**Mark Buchanan**, author of *The Rest of God*

"The message of holiness has been proclaimed throughout the centuries, though at times it has been distorted by legalism and misunderstanding. Bernie Van De Walle brings this important understanding of God's character back into the center of conversation in the life of the church. *Rethinking Holiness* provides a necessary, contemporary expression of a vital doctrine."

—**Carla Sunberg**, Nazarene Theological Seminary

"Van De Walle strikes at the heart of what God desires for the church and what Christians have always yearned for—holiness. He eloquently unravels the complex meaning of holiness and persuasively argues that Christians and non-Christians alike have a deep desire and need to be holy. *Rethinking Holiness* challenges those who have dismissed holiness as an antiquated and uninteresting topic to rethink their dismissal. This book offers deeply theological yet practical insights from a scholar who is passionate about helping ordinary Christians rediscover the essence of holiness."

—**Antipas L. Harris**, Regent University; author of *Holy Spirit, Holy Living: Toward a Practical Theology of Holiness*

RETHINKING
HOLINESS

RETHINKING
HOLINESS

A THEOLOGICAL
INTRODUCTION

BERNIE A. VAN DE WALLE

Baker Academic
a division of Baker Publishing Group
Grand Rapids, Michigan

© 2017 by Bernie A. Van De Walle

Published by Baker Academic
a division of Baker Publishing Group
P.O. Box 6287, Grand Rapids, MI 49516-6287
www.bakeracademic.com

Printed in the United States of America

Library of Congress Cataloging-in-Publication Data is on file at the Library of Congress, Washington, DC.

ISBN 978-0-8010-3067-3

17 18 19 20 21 22 23   7 6 5 4 3 2 1

In keeping with biblical principles of creation stewardship, Baker Publishing Group advocates the responsible use of our natural resources. As a member of the Green Press Initiative, our company uses recycled paper when possible. The text paper of this book is composed in part of post-consumer waste.

For Jean, Bunty, Michael, and Deanie,
each of whom taught me the values
of dedication, hospitality, and family,
and each of whom was gone long
before I would have preferred

Contents

Preface

A number of years ago, the president of my denomination, The Christian and Missionary Alliance in Canada, invited me to lead a seminar on the doctrine of holiness at one of our denomination-wide assemblies. At first I thought that he was simply seeking to have us tip our hats to our denominational heritage, a history related to the wider Holiness movement that grew out of the late nineteenth century. I fully expected that the seminar would be populated only by the "gray hairs" or those with an overdeveloped sense of historic obligation, which is to say that I expected the attendance to be small. After all, it seemed to me that the topic of holiness, even in those circles where sanctification has historically played a significant role, was out of fashion. Much to my surprise, there was a large turnout to the seminar, and many wanted to linger long after the allotted time to talk further and more deeply about holiness. Consequently, I proposed a course on the theology of holiness at Ambrose University, where I have served on the faculty since 1999. As with the seminar, I have been surprised to find enrollment in this course consistently about four times as high as any other elective course that I teach. This is true even though the other courses examine topics that would seem more provocative and popular than the topic of holiness. Together these experiences led me to conclude that there is a widespread hunger for knowledge and experience of the holy, even though it is often presented as being passé.

One of the major hurdles that I have encountered in teaching a course on holiness is a fundamental and popular misconception regarding the nature of Christian holiness. For the greatest majority of my students, holiness is understood to be a commodity, a lifestyle, or an ethic that one is expected to attain. My students thus assume that the course will be a how-to course designed to give them the steps or secrets to attaining holiness. Yet I have always been convinced that this is not the direction that the course should take but that students instead need to rethink their assumptions about theology before moving to practical matters. Thus we investigate the *nature* of Christian holiness. In time, students become intrigued and energized by the thought that holiness or "the holy" (as Rudolf Otto called it) is not primarily a code of conduct or kind of behavior but more basically a reference to God himself and only derivatively a reference to ethics. Rather than approaching holiness as a moral or legal category, we explore it as a divine, theological, or theocentric category. It has to do with God and what he is like. We can correctly understand the relation of holiness to ethics and morality only when we first understand it theologically.

This book is written out of that conviction. If the reader is looking for a how-to book or a book on ethics and morality, the market is replete with those. This book instead presents holiness as a category of theology proper. It is a "what-is" book. At the same time, rather than writing as if this were a highly technical theological treatise, I have written in a style that I trust will be more accessible to students, pastors, and the interested person in the pew. (Those who desire to dig deeper into this topic can consult my endnotes, which include the majority of my interaction with secondary literature.) My broader goal for the book is to aid the seeming renaissance of interest in holiness both inside and beyond the walls of the church.

To that end, I begin the book by identifying signs that indicate that there currently exists a broad desire and a great need for holiness. Somewhat surprisingly and perhaps counterintuitively, these signs can be found among Christians *and* among those outside the church. Yet, as I also discuss in chapter 1, a number of hurdles need to be overcome within the church and in wider society if holiness is to experience a true renaissance.

In the next two chapters I present a definition of holiness that is grounded in Scripture and Christian theology rather than in human intuition and reason. In chapter 2 I highlight some key insights from the Old and New Testaments and their surrounding cultural contexts—the ancient Near East for the Old Testament and the Greco-Roman world and first-century Judaism for the New Testament. Drawing from these insights, I conclude chapter 2 with my definition of holiness as *the transcendence or absolute otherness that is basic to God's being*. In chapter 3 I unpack this definition theologically by providing a closer look at the nature of God. I acknowledge that the popular understanding of God's holiness as moral perfection is true, but I argue that this moral aspect of holiness is secondary to the more fundamental aspect of transcendence. I then describe the relationship of God's holiness to other aspects of his nature, or divine attributes. I conclude by arguing that, when rightly understood, holiness is properly attributable only to God. All other forms of holiness are derivative and constantly dependent on their relation to the absolute holiness of God.

In the next four chapters I consider how this understanding of holiness affects other central theological categories. Chapter 4 explores the relationship between holiness and theological anthropology, considering what it means theologically to be human, especially in light of the fact that humans are created in the *imago dei*, the image of God. I argue that since humanity is created in God's image and since holiness is essential to God's being, holiness must in some way be an essential characteristic of humanity. From this fundamental insight I explore the possibilities and extent of human holiness. In chapter 5 I consider the relationship between holiness and the Christian doctrine of sin. I note that an accurate understanding of sin is necessary for any discussion of holiness since one's understanding of sin influences one's understanding of holiness and provides direction for one's pursuit of holiness.

In chapter 6 I explore the relation between holiness and salvation. I argue that a truncated theology of salvation—focused exclusively on the initial work of God in the life of believers (regeneration or justification) and limited only to a future realization—limits our understanding of holiness. I suggest that a holistic theology of salvation not only involves a change of one's *status* but also builds toward a change in one's *nature*. From this understanding of salvation, holiness is seen not only as the *hope* of salvation (fulfilled eschatologically) but also as the *means* of salvation. In chapter 7 I argue that holiness is fundamentally related to the church and that the holiness of any individual believer is necessarily grounded in the community that is one, *holy*, catholic, and apostolic. Moreover, rather than viewing each of these marks of the church as discrete, I argue that the church's holiness is seen precisely in its unity, catholicity, and apostolicity. The church manifests holiness in its peculiarity, its mission and ethic, and its dependence on the Triune God. To close chapter 7, I argue that for the church to be the church, its holiness must be not only real but also active and visible. In the concluding chapter, I reiterate the essential role that a proper understanding of holiness plays in its pursuit and summarize the key aspects of a Christian understanding of holiness.

At the end of each chapter, I offer a brief excursus on a theological or historical matter of relevance to the chapter. These topics include the hurdles we face in our pursuit of holiness (chap. 1), the role of Scripture as a foundation for our understanding of holiness (chap. 2), the relationship between human language and God's nature (chap. 3), the relationship between moral perfection and human innocence and limitations (chap. 4), the question of how to preach and practice holiness in a culture that values political correctness and tolerance (chap. 5), the distinction between improper understandings of holiness (legalism and license) and the biblical understanding of Christian liberty (chap. 6), and the story of the Donatists, an early Christian movement whose emphasis on holiness became distorted to the point of heresy (chap. 7). My hope is that these excurses will be a helpful feature of the book, providing a fuller texture and context to our discussion of holiness.

This book is not the product of a solitary individual. While I am solely responsible for any shortcomings it may possess, I am deeply indebted to the contributions of many, many others. First, my thanks go to President Gordon T. Smith and the Board of Governors of Ambrose University, who provided me with a sabbatical to begin work on this book in earnest. I also thank my colleagues at Ambrose who picked up my responsibilities while I was away. In addition, I am grateful to Michael Palmer, former dean of Regent University's School of Divinity, who invited me to spend my sabbatical with his faculty as Scholar-in-Residence. The feedback I received from Regent's faculty during the early stages of this work was invaluable. I also extend thanks to Pastor Peter Daley and the congregation of New Hope Christian Fellowship in Virginia Beach, who took me in and made me feel like part of their family while I was away from my own. Finally, and most important, I am deeply grateful to my own family—Colleen, David, and Ken—each of whom not only had to take on extra responsibilities while I was away on sabbatical but continued to do so even when I returned home and worked to (finally!) bring this project to completion. To everyone who made this book possible, please accept my sincerest thanks.

1

The Desire and Need for Holiness

I am a bit of a pack rat. While I have not reached hoarder status, I continue to hold on to a lot of things for which I have no current use. The only value these items have is sentimental, and sometimes even that is questionable. Among this growing pile of keepsakes, my most prized possession is the navy blue, nylon jacket I was issued when I made the baseball team in the second grade. At first I wore that jacket everywhere. I wore it at home. I wore it at school. I wore it at the dinner table. On more than one occasion, I wore it to bed. I even have a vague recollection of trying to wear it in the bath, but I am pretty sure my mother would have put a stop to that. That jacket and I were inseparable. When I was in the second grade, it meant the world to me; even now it continues to mean a lot. Yet today its well-worn frame sits in a chest with other memorabilia from my life: newspaper clippings, pennants, medals, shirts, and my high school letterman jacket. I love to keep that little blue jacket

1

close by. I can't imagine ever bringing myself to get rid of it even though I and my kids have long outgrown it. So there it sits in a chest in the hallway, an artifact from days gone by but with no impact on my current day-to-day life. It means a lot to me, but I rarely ever see it.

Holiness, even in the church, may seem to be something from a bygone era. Yet in the late nineteenth century, something called the Holiness movement deeply impacted the North American landscape. Its practical and unceasing emphasis on holiness deeply influenced both the church and general culture, and its impact was felt far and wide. It was, one could say, the height of fashion. All sorts of people "wore" their holiness wherever they went. They wore it to church. They wore it at work. They wore it at home. They wore it everywhere. It meant the world to them.

Today an emphasis on holiness seems to have all but disappeared not only from general society but even in the church. Every once in a while we pull it out of storage, talk about how important and great it was, and then put it back. We behave either as though holiness is out of fashion or as though we have outgrown its usefulness. The truth, however, is that holiness is never out of fashion. It is not passé. It does not belong to a bygone era. Quite the opposite is true. Those who have eyes to see will note that not only is holiness still useful, but it is also as "fashionable" as it ever was. As counterintuitive as it may seem, there currently exists a growing desire and need for holiness.

The Current Desire for Holiness

It should not be surprising that some people in any given era, including the present one, long for holiness. But what I am asserting is that there is more than just a longing. The current desire for holiness is not something that is held by a select few but is rather, in a categorical sense, *universal*. In one way or another, it is found everywhere. The desire for holiness is held by those within the church, by those outside the church, and especially by God.

Desire within the Church

The desire for holiness among many within the church can be seen in six forms:

1. The move to ancient and countercultural forms of worship.
2. The move to a holistic gospel that is concerned not only with one's eventual destiny and with one's soul but also with one's present life and with the whole of one's being.
3. The rejection of isolationism and the renewal of evangelical activism.
4. The attempt to see God.
5. The desire to have God in Christ seen through the church.
6. The scrutiny of various generations and groups by one another.

Each of these forms is discussed below.

Ancient Worship

Much has been made in recent years of the number of Christians, young and old alike, who find themselves increasingly attracted to worship styles other than those in which they were raised. Particularly, there seems to be a tendency among many evangelicals, again young and old alike, to participate in worship styles that are ancient, more liturgical, and consequently countercultural in style. There is a growing appreciation of forms of worship that evangelicals have traditionally considered obsolete at best and demonic at worst. One could even argue that these forms of worship are in part the very practices from which evangelicalism initially sought to free itself.

Yet those who are leaving behind contemporary evangelical worship for more ancient forms recognize that the goals of these two models of worship are significantly different. The primary goal of the liturgy to which they are drawn is *faithfulness*: faithfulness to the commands and instructions of Scripture, faithfulness to the historical liturgical practice of the church, and faithfulness to the nature of the God it professes to worship. They would argue that the goals of the worship style they are leaving behind—the contemporary evangelical model—is a well-meaning but misdirected acceptance of the culture's tastes and priorities. They would argue that instead of flowing from a desire to be faithful, contemporary evangelical worship flows from a desire to be acceptable: acceptable to the culture, acceptable to the unbeliever, and acceptable to one's personal preferences. Consequently, contemporary worship services that are understood to be most effective are often casual, familiar, frenetic, loud, conceptual, and complex. In response, the worship that many desire and seek out is formal, mysterious, peaceful, quiet, symbolic, and simple.

While much has been written about this trend, Robert Webber's books, including *Evangelicals on the Canterbury Trail*, *The Younger Evangelicals*, and his Ancient-Future series, are deeply respected and have served as both a stimulus to and a barometer of this trend.[1] Another sign of the trend toward the liturgical is the relatively recent publication of the multivolume *Ancient*

Christian Commentary on Scripture, edited by Methodist theologian Thomas C. Oden. That this series, which assembles the interpretations of the church fathers on the entirety of Scripture, is published by a historically evangelical publisher is further evidence of this trend among evangelicals.[2]

This trend is at least in part a rejection of the perceived accommodation of much of evangelical church life, including its forms of and goals for worship, to the character of the contemporary secular society. Rather than being something that flows from the history of the church, the character of the God being worshiped, or the biblical instructions on what is proper and fitting, contemporary evangelical worship is perceived to be a reflection of the tastes and priorities of the culture. Those who move to more liturgical forms of worship seek to find room for what they understand to be biblical virtues and practices not embraced—and sometimes even rejected outright—by the current church culture: holiness and mystery. They are thus drawn to practices such as silence, the use of images, and the regular practice of the Eucharist, which are central to a liturgical service but are looked on with grave suspicion by many contemporary evangelicals.

A Holistic Gospel

Throughout the ages Christians have been tempted to understand their faith not only as one that is interested in humanity's spiritual welfare but often as one that is *solely* interested in such. While such teaching has repeatedly been shown to be out of alignment both with the Scriptures and with orthodox Christian theology, it has proved to be resilient. In spite of its high view of Scripture and its emphasis on sound theology, evangelicalism has been particularly susceptible to this error.

It often has placed such an emphasis on the state of one's soul that it has inversely devalued caring for the state of one's physical welfare. In some circles, if one were to express concern for someone's living conditions and health, that person might be branded a "liberal" and thereby dismissed or even opposed.

This emphasis on the state of one's soul—and its resulting overemphasis on the future aspect of salvation—can be seen in the methods of evangelism sometimes employed by evangelicals in the twentieth century and still today. For example, Evangelism Explosion, an evangelism program that was popular in the latter half of the twentieth century, leads the would-be evangelist to set the stage for the realization of salvation as an event in the future, particularly in the throne room of God after one's death. It is here (and seemingly here alone) that salvation finds its payoff, as one is ushered into heaven. With such an emphasis on one's eternal destiny, such approaches show little understanding of, and therefore little concern for, the consequences that God's saving work may have here and now.[3]

Recently, however, there has been a resurgence of interest in what might be called a holistic anthropology—an understanding of humans as complex beings, composed of both the physical and the spiritual. According to this view, both aspects are essential to humanity. Moreover, these two aspects are understood to be deeply integrated and therefore inseparable from each other—or at least less readily and neatly separable as has often been thought.[4] One needs to go no further than the incarnation of Jesus to realize that true humanity is composed of that which is both spiritual and physical; to deny that the physical is essential to humanity is to deny the effectiveness and necessity of the incarnation. Evangelicals are increasingly adopting such a holistic anthropology and thereby rejecting an understanding of humanity that elevates the spiritual at the expense of the physical.

One might wonder what all of this has to do with holiness. First, we must remember that God's purpose in creating humanity was to have humans relate to him. As the Shorter Catechism of the Westminster Confession of Faith expresses it, humanity's "chief aim is to glorify God, and to enjoy him forever."[5] Second, Scripture repeatedly reminds us that God created the human as both physical and spiritual (e.g., 1 Thess. 5:23; Heb. 4:12). Furthermore, this complex being—this being of body and spirit—was part of what God pronounced "very good." At the very least, this pronouncement meant that God recognized that the being he created was well-suited to the purpose for which he created it—namely, to relate to him. While one might suggest that the physical nature of humanity may be superfluous to this God-given purpose, the teaching of Jesus in Mark 12:30 (referencing Deut. 6:5) suggests otherwise. According to Jesus, the most important commandment is that we love God with the entirety of our being—our heart, our soul, our mind, and our strength. Our love is not to come solely from that which is spiritual. If humans were created to relate to God in such a holistic fashion, then doing anything less cannot be considered good or whole or holy.

Evangelical Activism

In its pursuit of holiness, the church often finds it necessary to isolate itself from the balance of society, knowing that "bad company corrupts good character" (1 Cor. 15:33). Yet the church's understandable and obedient caution in regard to its interaction with the world has sometimes mutated into a condemnation of the world. The church's ministry to the world moved from being one that was *insulated*, taking appropriate steps to avoid contamination, to one that was *isolated*, avoiding contact of any kind by ensuring a constant distance from the world. This even included a growing isolation from other Christians whose orthodoxy or piety were possibly suspect. Historically, some have labeled this view "come-outism," a term used in reference to various movements that sought to detach themselves not only from the world but also from other Christians whose theological opinions and ethical positions were thought to be beneath their own.[6] I have often called this approach "cultural fundamentalism," a separation from fellowship with any who do not live to the same high standards that we believe we do.

Currently, there exists a movement within these historically isolationist churches that rejects the seemingly holier-than-thou attitude of a previous cultural fundamentalism that refused to dirty its hands or compromise its character by involving itself in the world or its problems. While still striving to protect their own integrity of life and belief, such groups are engaging the world. Realizing that the world is no longer beating down the doors of the church to discover what it has to say, these people are venturing onto the turf of the world—including previously forbidden places such as theatres, clubs, and pubs—in order "to seek and to save the lost" (Luke 10:19).

These same people also dismiss what has often been an attendant quietism that was willing to stand back, do nothing, and allow the world to hurtle toward its destruction (and sometimes to watch the destruction with an almost demonic glee). Instead, while realizing that the task of altering the world's trajectory is gargantuan, this recent movement is committed to doing all it can to resist the world's downward spiral.

The older isolationist and quietist approaches lacked a critical understanding of either contemporary society or its own cultural trappings. They were based on a move that failed to distinguish between *separation*, which is at the heart of holiness, and *isolation*, which is not. While separation is the command of God and in a certain way the essence of the church, the church is nevertheless called to live and minister *in* the world, even as the church is not *of* the world.

The Attempt to See God

During the Reformation of the sixteenth century, Martin Luther (1483–1546) "rediscovered" the doctrine of justification by faith alone—*sola fide*—through his reading of Scripture, particularly that of Romans 1:17.[7] In short, this doctrine asserts that people are not saved by the number or the excellence of their moral or religious works that are intended to garner favor with God. Rather, the salvation of humanity can come only from the merits of Christ. Salvation is not *gained*; it may only be *received*. It is appropriated only by the believers who place their faith in Christ. Religious and moral works, Luther argued, have nothing to do with obtaining salvation, which is received *sola gratia*—by grace alone, not by works.

While Luther and the other Reformers were correct in regard to *sola fide* and *sola gratia*, there has been a regular misunderstanding of these doctrines ever since. Rather than simply understanding that religious and moral works do not *merit* salvation, many have assumed that there is *no relationship at all* between works and salvation. But this raises the question: If there is no relationship between the two, why should someone be concerned with religious and moral works at all? On the chance that works might get in the way of *sola fide* and *sola gratia*, maybe they should be avoided altogether!

Yet there is a growing awareness among many evangelicals of the waywardness of this kind of thinking, including the Red Letter Christians and the Wesleyan Holiness Connection.[8] While Scripture teaches that salvation is received through faith alone and by grace alone (Eph. 2:8–9), there are numerous commands in Scripture for God's people to pursue holiness (e.g., Lev. 11:44–45; 19:2; 20:7, 26; Heb. 12:14; 1 Pet. 1:15–16; 2 Pet. 3:14). Many within the church today are seeking to take seriously these biblical commands to holiness. While there remains a commitment to the historic and central doctrines of the Reformation regarding the relationship between human works and salvation, many reject an understanding of salvation that finds not only its center but its entirety in justification by faith alone. Evangelicals are beginning to acknowledge that God has repeatedly commanded his people to be holy and that he expects it from them. Again, this pursuit of holiness is not to merit salvation but is instead based on the pursuit of God. As Jesus states in his Sermon on the Mount, the pure in heart are blessed, "for they will see God" (Matt. 5:8; cf. Luke 6; Heb. 12).

The Desire to Have God in Christ Seen

Within evangelicalism there is a tendency to separate Christ from his church. While the reasons for this may be many, the greatest is undoubtedly based on the perception that the character of Christ (sinless, loving, patient, etc.) and that of the church (sinning, judgmental, impatient, etc.) are not only different but also radically so. The temptation is to protect the reputation of Christ by distancing him from the church and to regularly highlight the distinctions between them.

Some are beginning to realize, however, that this convenient separation of Christ and the church is not possible without doing damage both to the church's teaching regarding the nature of Christ and to its teaching regarding the church itself, the body of Christ.[9] They acknowledge that the New Testament's portrayal of Christ is frequently associated with his people, the church. Rather than denying or diminishing Scripture's associations, they work to reform the church so that it might more accurately portray Christ to the world around it. To do so, they seek to appropriate a fuller understanding of the work of both the gospel and evangelism. They realize that the need of humanity is not merely cognitive or epistemic—it is not merely to know or to understand something that it did not know or understand before. It is more than just a change of mind or opinion. Rather, the saving work of Christ reforms the whole person, changing one's mind and the whole of one's being, including one's character.[10] Christians are thus called to be a different kind of people, which means that the reformation of the church to more accurately reflect Christ is essential to presenting the gospel to the world.

Interestingly, while this latter group has a different approach from those who create a sharp separation between Christ and the church, the approaches of both groups are grounded in the conviction that the watching world equates the character of the church with the character of Christ. The first group seeks to deny the relationship or at least severely qualify it; the second grants the relationship and asserts that it is a reality attested to in Scripture. Rather than denying the relationship, this latter group takes it seriously and actively embraces it. It realizes that the world's critique of the church in light of its nature and calling in Christ is accurate; consequently, it believes that the answer to the problem is to conform the church to the one Scripture says it is saved to be like: the Son (Rom. 8:27).

Mutual Scrutiny within the Church

Another way that the desire for holiness is visible within the church is the mutual scrutiny of the various generations within it. Each generation within the church is being watched by the others, and each expects the others to display holiness in ways appropriate to their context. Younger people look to their elders for leadership in this area, observing them for both cues and cautions. Older folk observe the younger generation, hoping to find within them the continuing marks of a youthful fervor for holiness. There are, of course, dangers to this kind of mutual scrutiny. Some older folk may become legalistic, seeking to pounce on the youth at the first sign of failing. (And lest we fool ourselves, we should acknowledge that some young people are just as strident as their older counterparts!) Yet many older folk pray for, encourage, and invest their lives and their resources in the younger people of their churches, enabling the youth to continue—and at times even surpass—the experiences of holiness by the older generations. Contrary to common belief, it is not simply the older folk watching the younger crowd. The scrutiny goes both ways.

Desire outside the Church

One might concede that there is a desire for holiness within the church—as there ought to be!—but still question whether that desire goes beyond the walls of the church. Evidence suggests that even though it might not always be rightly motivated or even rightly directed, a desire for holiness does indeed exist beyond the church's walls. This should not be surprising. Over sixteen hundred years ago, North African bishop Augustine wrote that God has "made us for [himself] and our hearts find no peace until they rest in [him]."[11] If he was right, then it is only natural that each and every one of us yearns for holiness, even if that yearning is often misdirected. Humanity was designed for the singular purpose of communing with God. Therefore, we should not be surprised when even those who are not Christian in some way desire holiness.

The desire for holiness manifests itself in a number of ways outside the church, of which three are mentioned:

1. The pursuit of spirituality.
2. The demand for the church to be what it says it is—that is, for the church to show integrity.
3. The call for the church to be what it was made to be— namely, salt and light.

Each of these are discussed below.

Pursuit of Spirituality

While theological and biblical studies have existed for centuries, the study of religion is a relatively recent phenomenon, a child of the nineteenth century. For the most part, the study of religion in the nineteenth and twentieth centuries identified the heart of all human religious endeavors, no matter their contexts, as the fascination with what Rudolph Otto called "the idea of the holy."[12] According to the study of religion, the holy is the focus not only of Christianity but of all religions. While this observation may be simplistic, it is not without a measure of truth. Fascination with and pursuit of the holy can be seen around the world, even in supposedly secular North American and European contexts.

Not missing the opportunity to cash in on this appetite for the holy, all sorts of vendors offer a wide variety of spiritualities and spiritual practices. Even if they are incorrectly motivated and aimed, these various behaviors, practices, methods, and products for attaining holiness are aggressively promoted and marketed. More important, they are widely purchased and employed. Such spiritual products and practices are as widely diverse as they are familiar—including such things as diets, yoga, and philosophies that are represented by celebrities like Tom Cruise, Tony Robbins, Deepak Chopra, and Oprah Winfrey. Together such "gurus" generate billions of dollars of revenue every year from the growing spirituality market.

About a decade ago William Paul Young published his novel *The Shack*, which has since sold nineteen million copies and is currently available in no fewer than thirty languages.[13] Such a response to a self-published book by an obscure author is another manifestation of the desire for holiness. Young's message about a God who is moved by people's circumstances and seeks to relate intimately to them has profoundly influenced the spiritual understanding of countless Christians; yet the level and breadth of *The Shack*'s success cannot be explained by its popularity within the church alone. Sales of that kind demand that its popularity—and that an interest in holiness—has reached far beyond the traditional confines of the church.

Demand for Integrity within the Church

Those beyond the walls of the church may not be well-versed in its doctrines and practices, but the church's ministry

has at least been successful enough to give most people beyond its walls the impression that the church has holiness
as its goal, even if often fails to meet this goal. Whether the
church likes it or not, the world has every right to expect and
demand that the church live up to its own calling. This is
especially true given the very vocal critiques that the church
has launched (sometimes rightly, sometimes wrongly) against
others. If the church is going to criticize others for certain
behaviors, those others are right to demand that the church
make sure its own house is in order in those areas—or at the
very least to earnestly strive to overcome its failures. As Jesus
taught and the world expects, the church cannot diagnose the
speck in the eyes of others without first addressing the plank
in its own (Matt. 7:3). The church cannot rail against certain
behaviors—divorce, greed, sexual deviance—and at the same
time behave no differently in these very same areas.[14] Those
outside the church are well within their rights to demand such
integrity within the church. But, interestingly, by so demanding
moral integrity within the church, such critics demonstrate
their own desire for holiness, for consistency between words
and actions.

The Call for the Church to Be Salt and Light

Jesus taught that the church must not hide its light under a
bushel but be salt and light to the world (Matt. 5:13–16; cf. Luke
8:16–18). While some outside the church would like nothing
more than for the church to hide its light, many more desire
for the church to be salt and light in the world. This is true
particularly among those outside the church who are interested
in issues of social welfare, including the care for the poor and
disenfranchised. There is a growing interest among those who

15

are not Christian to work alongside those who are on those matters where they are in agreement, even if their interest arises from significantly different places.

In some countries that philosophically separate the state and the church, government agencies are approaching the church to partner with it to provide and to manage services for the poor, the elderly, and the marginalized. Some countries are willing accept church people as volunteers and even to call on them to provide leadership and direction in these areas. The Salvation Army's worldwide ministry to the destitute and marginalized may be the best known of these kinds of works. In North America and abroad, it regularly receives both invitations to be involved in local crises and resources from state agencies to do its humanitarian work. Samaritan's Purse, an evangelical relief agency associated with the Billy Graham Evangelistic Association, often cooperates with government agencies at home and abroad to bring disaster relief to those in greatest need.

The Desire of God

The third party who desires holiness is none other than God: the Holy One. From Genesis through Revelation and almost every place in between, Scripture is clear that God desires a holy people (e.g., 2 Cor. 6:16–18). Moreover, it is equally clear that God has worked, is working, and will work toward that end (e.g., Eph. 5:25–27). God's plan for a holy people, which we refer to with terms such as "salvation" and "redemption," speaks not only to the *transportation* of humanity (from a destiny of eternal punishment to a place of eternal joy) but, more important, to the *transformation* of humanity (from their current condition to the kind of people God intends them to be). The salvation that God has made possible is not primarily interested in altering humanity's location; it is focused on altering its very being.

The incarnation, death, and resurrection of Jesus Christ demonstrate the extent to which God was willing to go to achieve this transformation of humanity. As the renowned nineteenth-century Cambridge theologian Handley C. G. Moule once wrote, "It is nothing less than the supreme aim of the Christian Gospel that we should be holy; that the God of peace should sanctify us through and through our being, that we should 'walk worthy of the Lord unto all pleasing' (1 Thess. 5:23)."[15]

The Current Need for Christian Holiness

We have seen that the desire for holiness is widespread. It is found among those inside and outside the church, and it is certainly true of God. When speaking about desire, I am talking about that inward longing for something that is currently absent or at least not present in the quantity or quality that one would like. But if desire implies absence or lack, then the desire for holiness we observed in the previous section suggests that there is a need for it. That need is addressed in this section.

Of course, while desire often indicates need, there are many things we might desire that we don't truly need. When I talk about need, then, I am talking about that which we cannot survive without. I am not referring just to something we would really like or something that would satisfy some longing. On the one hand, if I were to exclaim "I *need* a Coke!" one would assume that I probably mean something more like "I have a strong desire for a Coke!" On the other hand, if I shouted "I need a drink of water!" it *might* simply be an expression of a strong desire, but, given the human constitution, it could just as well indicate that a drink of water is necessary for my survival. In the latter sense, what is needed is something that is essential not only for pleasure but also for life itself. Below I argue that holiness is not merely the desire of many but the need of all—that it is something we cannot do without, not only for our well-being but also for our very lives. This need can be seen both within and outside the church.

Need within the Church

Holiness is needed within the church in four ways:

1. Holiness is necessary to see God.
2. Holiness is necessary for the church to be the church.
3. Holiness is necessary for the church's integrity.
4. Holiness is necessary for the church to do what it was created to do.

Again, each is discussed below.

Holiness Is Necessary to See God

As discussed above, there has been a tendency among evangelicals to promote the Reformation doctrine of "justification by faith alone" in such a way that leaves no place or reason for the pursuit of holiness. If holiness has any place at all, it is understood to be little more than something we will receive once we get to heaven. While living a holy life here and now may be understood to have a few practical advantages, many contemporary evangelicals do not consider it to be a necessary aspect of the Christian life.

Yet on more than one occasion Scripture clearly connects holiness with the ability to see and commune with God. For example, Hebrews 12:14 states, "Make every effort to live in peace with everyone *and to be holy*; without holiness no one will see the Lord" (emphasis added). This passage does not allow us to assume that this holiness is either the holiness of Christ who indwells the church or the position that the church holds because of its relationship to God. This passage is written to those who were already indwelt by Christ and who were already God's people. Yet it nevertheless exhorts its readers to pursue peace and holiness. The holiness being encouraged here cannot be something these people already possessed—at least not fully. And to make matters even more serious, this verse attaches a significant consequence to the failure to pursue holiness: "without holiness no one will see the Lord." While there is no doubt that humanity is justified by faith alone, this verse reminds us that there is a necessary role for the pursuit of holiness in the Christian life.

Holiness Is Necessary for the Church to Be the Church

There are probably as many different understandings of what the church is as there are understandings of what holiness is. Some churches are distinguished by their form of government, whether they are led by bishops (episcopal), by a board of elders (presbyterian), or by some sort of democratic process (congregational). Other churches are distinguished by what they profess theologically—their creeds or statements of faith. Others are distinguished by the ethnicity of their members or by some kind of ties to their country of origin. Still others are distinguished by the particular mission to which they feel God has called them.

In spite of this wide variety of ways of viewing the church, there has been almost unanimous agreement that the church—no matter what its governmental, ethnic, or missional expressions may be—bears four marks. From the formation of the Nicene Creed in 325 (and likely even prior to that), the church has been understood to be "one, *holy*, catholic, and apostolic" (emphasis added). While the church may be identified by a number of characteristics, if it is to truly be the church, it must be holy. Holiness is one of the church's few essential characteristics. If it is not holy, it is not the church.

Holiness Is Necessary for the Church's Integrity

This point flows from the previous one. If the church is to be true to its nature as the body that is indwelled by the presence of God and true to its mission to reveal God to the world as his ambassadors, then it must live a life that properly reflects both that nature and that mission. Practically speaking, if the church and its message are each to be taken seriously, the church must be seen as striving toward holiness itself. While it may not always and fully achieve that goal, the church still must make every effort to do so. Before the eyes of a watching world, the church's earnest effort toward holiness will be noticed and appreciated. If the effort is not apparent, that too will be noticed and remembered. To present a message of holiness but not to live a life marked by that holiness rightly calls into question both the church's integrity and the nature or even the reality of the God whom it professes to worship. A church that preaches a certain message and that does not pursue the goals of that same message is rightly an object of mockery and disdain.

Holiness Is Necessary for the Church to Do What It Was Created to Do

The church has been given a mandate or, as it often prefers to call it, a mission. It is a lofty mission: not only to take the gospel to the ends of the earth but also to change the world as it does so. If the church hopes to fulfill this magnificent mandate, it will need to rally all the resources at its disposal. Rarely has the church thought of holiness as a resource, yet it most certainly is. Apart from simply providing the church with integrity, holiness is powerful in and of itself. The list of those whose holiness lent power to their ministry is long and significant. In addition to the ultimate example, Jesus Christ, we might think of people such as Francis of Assisi, Mother Teresa, and Billy Graham. Undoubtedly, each of these individuals was gifted in at least one way or another: evangelism, compassion, prophecy, and so on. Yet it is the character of their lives that serves as their greatest gift. While each may have had a measure of success apart from a life marked by holiness, their lives of holiness are why they will continue to be revered into perpetuity. If the church presently struggles or fails in the fulfillment of its mandate—to present Christ to the whole world—it is due in no small part to the church's lack of holiness in the pursuit of this end.

Need outside the Church

The need for holiness is not limited to the church. Though the reasons for the need of holiness differ from those within the church, there still exists a very real need for holiness by those outside the church, for at least two reasons:

1. Holiness is necessary for the world to be effectively and powerfully evangelized.

21

2. Holiness is necessary for the world to be able to see God.

As will become apparent, I am not saying that everyone outside the church would admit to these needs—much less that they would agree with the reasons I provide for these needs. Denying that one has needs, however, is nothing new. People sometimes even deny their need for things as basic and universal as shelter, food, clothing, and love. Denying they need such things does not prove that they do not need them. In the same way, those outside the church who deny their need for holiness do not disprove their need for holiness; rather, their denial attests to the fact that they do not know themselves or their situations as well as they think they do.

Holiness Is Necessary for the World to Be Evangelized

If the world is going to be reached with the gospel, which may be its greatest need, it needs holiness. However, the holiness the world needs comes not from the world but rather from the church. The reason is simple: as noted earlier, the message of the evangelist is more credible, more compelling, and therefore more readily received by those who are convinced (and who can convince others) that this same gospel has had a life-changing effect on the life of the one proclaiming it. A salesman who does not display the purported advantages of his product in his own life will not be able to convince many of the necessity, quality, and usefulness of his product. Likewise, a church that does not display the holiness that it says is central both to its own identity and to its message will not convince many of the truth of its message.

22

Holiness Is Necessary for the World to See God

Scripture tells us that God has shown us what he is like through the kind of world he has created (Ps. 19:1; Rom. 1:20). The nature of the created order tells us something about the character of the One who created it. This is what theologians call *natural* or *general revelation*. It is self-disclosure of God that is set before everyone in all times and places. Yet God has also revealed himself more directly and in a more detailed manner than through general revelation. At various times and in various ways God has spoken directly to his people. Scripture records many of these instances, which theologians call *special revelation*. Since God has displayed himself in various ways through both general and special revelation, there is ample opportunity for humanity to see God, if only it will look.

The church may serve as yet another kind revelation of God. Indeed, this is its very mandate. In everything it does and says, the church should exhibit the holy character of God to those around it. This manner of revelation has two advantages possessed by neither general nor special revelation. First, the revealing work of the church is more active than the revealing work of both creation and Scripture. While creation and Scripture continually reveal the nature of God, they are not as able to actively engage people, to approach them directly with their message. The church is both able and mandated to do just this. It is to approach people and reveal God and his gospel to them. Second, the church is more able to interact and converse with the world. It is able to carry on a dialogue with its audience, to engage in a dynamic relationship of listening, speaking, and responding.

Ultimately those outside the church need to be holy themselves if they hope to see God. Humanity was originally created

23

for the singular purpose of living in intimate relationship with God. The current and universal human condition, however, is one of sin, the natural and necessary consequence of which is separation from God. If humanity is to see God, to be in relationship with him, it is necessary that its sinful situation change. To see God requires holiness, which by its very nature is both the antithesis to and the cure for sin. Without holiness, no one can see God; without God, one's destiny is very grave indeed. Before we can begin to address this holiness deficit, we must first know what we mean when we talk about holiness. In the next two chapters we will explore Scripture and Christian theology to develop our understanding of what holiness is.

EXCURSUS: **Hurdles to Holiness**

I am not so naive as to think that the contemporary desire and need for holiness are not without their challenges. Numerous and significant hurdles must be overcome. Each one in its own way threatens to derail what seems to be growing momentum in this area. Here we'll discuss five hurdles.

1. Many simply evade discussing holiness altogether. While the church may value and cherish holiness, it doesn't want to talk about it. It doesn't deny the importance of holiness; it just wants to steer clear of examining what it is and what it means. Jerry Bridges, author of the modern classic *The Pursuit of Holiness*, says Christians are unwilling to talk about holiness lest they either show their ignorance about what holiness is and how holiness works or, perhaps worse, come to realize their responsibility to live up to it.[16] It seems better to let the sleeping dog of holiness lie.

2. Some consider the whole idea of holiness to be an outdated concept. While it had its time and may have resulted in some really good things, that time is now past. The world in which it lived and was effective is gone. The contemporary world is substantially different and therefore requires a substantially different approach.

3. Some think holiness is nothing other than a quaint or innocuous term used to talk about what is an otherwise sinister, debilitating, and enslaving legalism—one that resists the good news of the grace of God and the believer's freedom in Christ. It is, in other words, a wolf in sheep's clothing; the pursuit of holiness is anything but what it seems to be. Rather than being something that elevates humanity, it is something that actually diminishes it.

4. Others think the pursuit of holiness does little more than further alienate and isolate the church from the world around it. The pursuit of holiness only develops within the church a holier-than-thou attitude that rejects and repulses the world around it. Consequently, rather than enabling the church's ministry, the pursuit of holiness limits any real influence it could have or any good it could do.

5. Still others note that the church cannot agree—could never agree!—on what holiness is, what it looks like, or what it does and does not do. Not only that, they point out that, rather than being good for the church as iron sharpens iron, these disagreements have led to deep-seated and lasting divisions within it.[17] If the church cannot agree on what holiness is, how it is received (or gained), or how it manifests itself, how on earth can the church expect to produce it?

This list of objections to the pursuit of holiness is impressive. It may even be daunting. Regrettably, it is not even exhaustive.

There is no doubt that significant hurdles stand in the way of an interest in and a revival of holiness. These hurdles cannot be ignored; they are not phantasms. To overcome these hurdles, we must first acknowledge their (partial) truths:

1. It is true that holiness is not a topic that Christians often discuss. Rarely, even in church circles, does one hear about the role of holiness in the Christian life. (The very opposite may be the case: while perhaps a nice topic for an occasional sermon, holiness has no essential role in the Christian life.)

2. It is true that the old forms of holiness may no longer be either relevant or appropriate to the current reality. We cannot assume that all we have to do to pursue or achieve holiness is to mimic the acts of the saints of the past. That simply will not do.[18]

3. It is true that some things that have posed as manifestations of holiness are nothing other than the burdensome yokes from which Jesus said he came to deliver us (Matt. 11:28–30).

4. It is also true that some understandings and forms of holiness have resulted in the unnecessary alienation of the church from the world. Too often the pursuit of holiness, which ought to be a humbling enterprise, has resulted in spiritual pride. This is contrary to true holiness, which flows from the character of God manifest in the person of Jesus Christ and thereby must be self-denying rather than self-aggrandizing.

5. Finally, it is true that there has never been agreement within the church about how to define holiness—at least not with any real precision. There has been even less agreement about how holiness is to be pursued and what it will look like when it does appear. Consequently, there has been significant debate and unfortunate division among those who have said that holiness, more than anything else, was their interest

and their pursuit. Holiness became something over which to divide rather than something around which to unite.[19]

This list of truths is far too long and far, far too pathetic. Yet in spite of these hurdles to holiness, the desire and need for holiness are as strong as they ever have been. Though contemporary examples of holiness seem rare, it is not because there is no demand for them. I would even suggest that the current desire and need for holiness are as great as—or even greater than—they were during the peak of the Holiness movement.

Due in part to these hurdles, holiness is in short supply today. Very few of us would claim that we have both pursued and attained a life of holiness with any significant measure of success. In response to others who claim to have attained holiness, we might assert that it would be nice if their lives were to show it. For most of us, the list of those we would identify as holy would be either very short or nonexistent.

One might argue that this lack of holiness (at least partially) proves that there is neither a desire nor a need for it. But as we've seen in this chapter, there are growing signs of a renewed desire and need for holiness. For many, then, removing these hurdles might be just what they need to pursue the holiness that they already desire and need.

2

A Biblical Definition of Holiness

Every student who has taken a course with me knows that one of my favorite movies is the 1987 comedic classic *The Princess Bride*.[1] My course lectures are peppered with quotes from it. In class students hear such familiar phrases as "Mawwiage!" "As you wish!" "Mostly dead," "You killed my father; prepare to die!" "Anybody want a peanut?" and "Have fun storming the castle!" One of the most memorable lines comes in reply to antagonist Vizzini's repeated use of the word "Inconceivable!" in response to a wide variety of incidents throughout the first half of the movie. Finally, one of his companions, Inigo Montoya, responds to Vizzini's constant and apparently indiscriminate use of this term. "You keep using that word," Montoya says to Vizzini with a quizzical look. "I do not think it means what you think it means."

Many of us, Christian and non-Christian alike, use the term "holiness" in a similar way. "Holiness" is one of those words we use—and in some Christian traditions use quite often—even though most of us would be hard pressed to define it with any depth, precision, or clarity. Yet if holiness is to be not only a subject of our study but also the object of our pursuit, and perhaps even that which fundamentally characterizes our way of life as Christians, then defining this concept is an absolute necessity. What we understand holiness to be will surely affect how we pursue it.

When it comes to hunting or fishing, what you hope to catch will determine where you go, when you go, and the kind of equipment you bring with you. In the same way, certain understandings of holiness require certain approaches and disqualify others. What we understand holiness to be and the way in which we hope to pursue it are inextricably related. Indeed, how we define holiness may even influence whether we believe that it is something that can be pursued at all. Some definitions of holiness make humans passive participants in the whole process. On the one hand, if holiness is solely the gracious gift of God, given only to those whom he has predetermined, then the whole idea of pursuing holiness is foolish. The most we can do is to wait and hope to receive it. On the other hand, if one defines holiness as something that is attained at least in part through human activity, then one would be wise to observe what God has said about how to successfully attain or obtain it. Ultimately, one must know what one is pursuing if there is to be any hope of success or even progress. Defining "holiness," then, is not just an academic exercise for ivory tower theologians. It is a practical necessity.

Scores of books in the Christian marketplace speak to the *how* and the *why* of holiness; that is, they seek to teach people how to pursue, engage, and perhaps even attain holiness. However, few books seriously consider the *what* of holiness; few books explore what we mean when we use this word. The purpose of this chapter—and, indeed, this book as a whole—is to address the fundamental question, what is holiness? To begin to answer this question, we turn to Scripture.

The Old Testament Portrayal of Holiness

The Ancient Near East

The wider world in which the Old Testament was written and in which the Israelites lived (often called the ancient Near East) was a deeply and thoroughly religious world that understood itself to be surrounded by the holy.[2] It was a world that spent lots of time and energy attending to the holy, even if its identification was inaccurate and its pursuit of holiness was wrongly directed. For this world, the holy was understood to be something—anything—that was out of the ordinary, different, or distinct, including things such as exceedingly large or old trees, strange geological formations, and oddly colored animals. Such mysterious things were objects of wonder and fascination, and on occasion they were also objects of fear and terror. Out of this wonder, fascination, and even fear developed a reverence for such objects.[3]

The word these people used to designate the notion of the holy was *qdš*. It was used primarily to designate anything that was different, distinct, unique, and therefore "separate."[4] Yet it always carried religious connotations.[5] In the ancient Near East there was not as clear of a distinction between the sacred and the secular as there is today, and so strange objects were often considered to have some kind of supernatural origin, explanation, or purpose. Everything that was understood not to be *qdš* was *hōl*—common, average, normal. What is sometimes difficult for modern people to grasp is that when these people called something *qdš* as opposed to *ḥōl*, they were not necessarily saying anything about its ethical or moral status. That is, *qdš* did not necessarily speak about goodness or righteousness. It simply referred to the object's distinctiveness, otherness, or difference.

Qdš was used in two different but related ways in the ancient Near East. First, as already noted, it denoted a realm or a sphere of existence that was distinct from the *ḥōl*.[6] This meant that *qdš* was also beyond common explanation and therefore at least to a degree unknown and perhaps even unknowable. This introduces to us the idea of the holy as the *transcendent*—that which is beyond the common, beyond the natural.

The second way *qdš* was used in the ancient Near East was more relational. Something might be considered to be *qdš* if it had passed through a process of dedication and consecration whereby the otherwise common thing (*ḥōl*) became intimately related to or belonged to something that was *qdš*.[7] While this rite of consecration was rarely, if ever, conducted by the holy thing itself, it resulted in the otherwise common thing or person being set apart for the use of and relationship with that which is *qdš*. The peoples of the ancient Near East thus believed that there could be holy persons, holy utensils, holy books, holy places, and so on—even if these things were never to be understood as having become *qdš* in and of themselves. Their holiness was constantly dependent on their relationship to that which was holy in and of itself.

Again, this understanding of the holy did not convey moral or ethical content.[8] Something that was understood to be *qdš* was not necessarily understood to be morally or ethically superior. For contemporary Christians who do not—indeed, cannot—

separate our understanding of holiness from our understanding of the God who is morally and ethically perfect, it can be difficult to disassociate our understanding of holiness from moral and ethical connotations. Yet, interestingly, while God is called "holy" hundreds of times in the Old Testament, nowhere in the Old Testament is God explicitly described as morally or ethically pure.[9]

Ancient Israel

When the Old Testament uses the word *qdš* in relation to the God of Israel, it describes his absolute and thorough distinction not only from the common (*ḥōl*) but also from every created thing. In other words, when the Old Testament describes the God of Israel as holy, it identifies him in a category unto himself. He is, literally, one of a kind. He is the One. He is the one and only Creator God. He alone is the source of everything else that is. When the Old Testament proclaims that the God of Israel is *qdš*, it asserts that he alone is truly God, that he is without peer or competitor.[10]

Yet, like its broader ancient Near Eastern usage, *qdš* is not primarily an ethical or moral descriptor in the Old Testament. While God is morally superior and ethically perfect, the Old Testament use of *qdš* does not denote such but instead primarily denotes the singularity of God's being. It asserts that God alone is God, that there are no other gods at all.

The picture of God as the Holy One is seen repeatedly throughout the Old Testament. For example, immediately following the miracle of the parting of the Red Sea and God's delivery of the children of Abraham from the hands of their Egyptian pursuers, the Israelites break into song, praising God and proclaiming his incomparable power. They sing about the amazing power of their

God in contrast to that of Egypt's so-called god, Pharaoh—a contrast that could not possibly make this Egyptian "deity" look more impotent.[11] At one point they sing, "Who among the gods is like you, O Lord? Who is like you—majestic in holiness, awesome in glory, working wonders?" (Exod. 15:11). Their question is rhetorical. In light of recent events, the obvious answer is "No one!" Only their God is truly God.

Similarly, God's holiness is proclaimed in a heavenly vision described in Isaiah 6. There the heavenly courtyard is vividly and dramatically described. With nothing other than the very presence of God to make the whole scene shake in reverence, the seraphim, those who serve constantly in the presence of God, cry out, "Holy, holy, holy is the LORD Almighty" (Isa. 6:3). The triple repetition of the word "holy" signifies both the perfection of God's holiness and his utter distinction from everything else. That is, it affirms not only that God is perfectly holy but also that he alone is such.

The clear teaching of the Old Testament is that God and God alone is worthy of worship (Exod. 20:3; 34:14; Deut. 5:7; 6:13–14; Ps. 96: 4–5; 2 Kings 17:35–36) This worship is due him because of his mighty deeds of creation and salvation. No other god—or rather nothing else that is regarded as a god—can measure up to this God. He is without peer or competitor. He alone is God. He alone is divine. He is in a category by himself. That is what makes him holy. Again, the designation of holiness, even when applied to the God of Israel, primarily refers to the nature of his being and is not tied to his morality. He is regarded as holy because there is no one, in either heaven or on earth, who is like him. In the Old Testament, as in the religions of the ancient Near East, holiness is not simply (or even primarily) an ethical category. It speaks primarily of transcendence.

The Old Testament also retains from the ancient Near East the relational understanding of holiness that was noted earlier. While holiness is the intrinsic property of God alone, persons, places, and things can come to be related to him through his consecrating touch, such that they too may be understood to be holy. There are many references throughout the Old Testament to things that are "holy" other than God: holy ground, a holy nation (Israel), the holy utensils of the tabernacle or temple, and so on. Such things are deemed holy not in and of themselves, however, but because they are in a particular relationship with God. They are holy because God has chosen them to be in a particular relationship with him who is in himself the Holy One.[12]

The New Testament Portrayal of Holiness

The Greco-Roman World

The Greco-Roman world in which the New Testament was written was, like the ancient Near East, a highly religious environment.[13] Religious activity was visible and integrated into every aspect of daily life: from meals and work to the military.[14] This environment was open-minded in regard to which religion—and there were many options—one should adhere. And it was not necessary to limit oneself to just one religion. One was free to pick and choose aspects of various religions that one found beneficial. In this setting, religion was not primarily about theological creeds or even ethical purity. Thus, as in the ancient Near East, so too in the Greco-Roman world holiness was not understood to be about morality. Instead, holiness was primarily identified with the exercise of power. Temples abounded and were crucial to public life. And while priests were highly regarded, it was not because of their high moral standing. Rather, they were revered for their ability, through the mastery of the religious rites and techniques, to manipulate the various deities for the benefit of their followers. Ritual, not creed and certainly not morality, was central to religious expressions.[15] When purity did come into play, it was ritual purity—whether one had prepared oneself properly according to the demands of the religion and completed the rite without error or omission—rather than moral purity or ethical holiness. Indeed, given the grossly immoral acts attached to many of the temple rites, moral purity as we would understand it may have even served as a hindrance to the effectiveness of the ritual.

First-Century Judaism

While first-century Jews were a religious people, they were not at all as liberal as the Romans in regard to their religious allegiances. Unlike the syncretistic Romans, the Jews were dedicated monotheists; they believed in the existence of only one God and worshiped him alone. Additionally, they had concrete ideas of what this God was like. First, like their Hebrew forebears, they were convinced that holiness is at the heart of God's nature. More than any other descriptor, holiness defines who God is. It is God's most distinguishing characteristic. While the word "holy" may be rightly used to designate things other than this God (e.g., priests, temples, ground), such derivative holiness is never independent or self-constituted; it is always dependent on an intimate relationship with the Holy One. Though this secondary holiness is real, it is a derived and constantly dependent holiness.[16]

Based on God's promise to their ancestor Abraham hundreds of years previously, first-century Jews understood themselves to be God's people (Gen. 12:2). They believed that they enjoyed a special relationship with him—that they were his holy people (Exod. 19:5–6). They also knew that as God's holy people they must reflect his holy character. Therefore, many within first-century Judaism were preoccupied with obtaining and maintaining their own holiness. This preoccupation often manifested itself in efforts to be distinct from the surrounding nations. They separated themselves, as much as they were able, from the people and the other cultures around them. Over time, however, their emphasis on separation—the proposed solution—became the problem. Rather than simply being distinct from those around them, many Jews practically isolated themselves from people in other cultures. While this may have enabled them to resist being negatively influenced by others, it also ensured that the Jews would have little influence on those who lived around them.

The Jews knew that God's choice of Abraham and his descendants was unexpected and unmerited. Neither Abraham nor his descendants earned or deserved God's decision to choose them. God simply chose them. They knew that God chose Abraham because God is gracious and merciful, not because of anything Abraham had done, and that they continued to be God's people only because of God's grace and mercy. Realizing that God had taken the initiative in establishing a relationship with Abraham and his descendants, and that when God had done so it was not at all based on their merit, they believed God would remain faithful to that relationship despite their failings. The relationship was established with an unworthy people, so their continued unworthiness would not serve as an insurmountable hurdle to the relationship's ongoing survival. Yet this did not mean there would be no consequences for the nation's failure to be faithful. The greatest of these consequences had been Israel's exile from the land God had promised to Abraham and their continued servitude to foreign powers.

God brought his people back to the Promised Land in the time of Ezra and Nehemiah (sixth century BCE), but in a very real sense their exile had not yet come to an end. Even though many of them were back in the land, it was plain to them that the land was neither theirs nor under their control. While they were back in the land, their return fell short of the promise God seemed to have made to them. They thus concluded that something must still be wrong.[17]

Given their dedication to the idea that holiness and righteousness were part of the unchanging character of God, Jews during this period—known as Second Temple Judaism (sixth century BCE to first century CE)—knew that occupation of the Promised Land by foreign powers could not be due to his unfaithfulness. The responsibility, they concluded, must be theirs. They reasoned that there must be ongoing and debilitating sin in their midst. To combat this, a number of holiness and renewal movements were born. Their goal was to stem Israel's sinful ways, to remedy its unfaithfulness, and to correct its straying. Various Jewish sects formed, each offering a different response to this problem. The Pharisees, for example, sought holiness by emphasizing the central role of the Old Testament laws and worked at defining and observing them scrupulously. Others, like the Essenes, sought holiness by promoting a communal life outside the mainstream of society, one marked by simplicity, austerity, and voluntary poverty. Still others believed that holiness would only arrive in the future with the long-anticipated arrival of a messiah, a national hero who would overthrow their oppressors and usher in the era of a new covenant, written on the hearts of the people. This new era would be never-ending and would even surpass the best days of the old covenant made with Abraham.[18]

In the midst of these diverse responses to foreign occupation, Jewish religious life focused on two pillars: the life and rites of the temple and the study of and adherence to the Scriptures (the Torah).[19] By the first century CE, the Romans had allowed the Jews to rebuild the hub of Jewish religious life, the temple, which was central to Jewish life in a number of ways. First, the temple was the only place where the Jews were authorized to offer the required sacrifices. Second, the temple was the national shrine, the symbol that represented the Jewish people. When one thought of the temple, one thought of the Jews—and vice versa. Third, the temple was one of the main places where the Jews congregated as a people. Finally, and most important, the Jews believed that it was in the temple—particularly in a place called the holy of holies—that God's presence was most fully manifest on earth.

First-century Jews also placed a strong emphasis on the Torah. The Torah, the Jewish Scriptures, told the story of God's covenant faithfulness to his people. Furthermore, they believed that careful attention to the Scriptures would provide insight into how God's people were to live their lives. The Torah, the Jews believed, contained the definition of what it meant to be the people of God and instructions for how to live properly as the people of God. First-century Jews understood holiness to be absolutely necessary for the kind of communion with God for which Israel was created. Through participation in the life of the temple and study and application of the Torah, they sought to be the kind of holy people God had intended them to be.

Christ—the Measure and Means of Holiness

One cannot consider the theology of holiness in the New Testament without considering how its central figure, Jesus Christ, shapes and determines this understanding. It is interesting that while the vision of the heavenly throne room in Isaiah 6 is awe-inspiring and vivid, and while the person of God is central to the whole scene, it contains no description of God himself. We know he is there (we are even told what he is wearing!), but God himself is not described. Of course, this is in keeping with the rest of the Old Testament where the God to whom we refer in song as "Immortal, Invisible, [and] Only Wise"[20] is beyond description. However, with the arrival of Jesus, the one who is "true God from true God" (to quote the Constantinopolitan Creed),[21] this God has a face. In the incarnation of Jesus, God takes on physical form. The New Testament records how the Holy One of Israel "became flesh" in Jesus Christ (John 1:14), "Immanuel," "God with us" (Matt. 1:23; cf. Isa. 7:14).

The incarnation is thus the means through which the Holy One is revealed to his creatures. But it is also a holy thing itself. The incarnation is holy because it is unique. It is transcendent. It is one of a kind. There is nothing else like it. It is incomparable. While we may seek to understand and explain it by comparing it to other things, all comparisons ultimately fail. The incarnation is a mystery. We have nothing from our common experience against which to measure it or by which to fully understand it. Undoubtedly, this is at least in part why so many attempts to understand the incarnation have ended up in error (heresy). Instead of allowing the incarnation to remain mysterious and in a sense "wild," efforts have been made to "tame" it.

In the incarnation Jesus, the one who is "true God from true God," became fully human. It is not just that Jesus appeared to be human or that he was only partially human. In the incarnation, God the Son took upon himself the fullness of what is essential to human being, yet he was without sin (Heb. 4:15). Jesus is both "true God from true God" and "fully human in every way" (Heb. 2:17). That means that when we look at Jesus, we see what God is like; and it is just as true that when we look at Jesus, we see what humanity is like. Indeed, we see the epitome of human being. Therefore, when we want to know what it means to be human, we should look not at ourselves, our peers, or our constructs of the best traits of the best of us. Instead, we are to look to Jesus.

Since, as discussed above, God is intrinsically holy, Jesus, as the one who is "very God of very God" is by his very nature holy. Yet the holiness of Jesus is not limited to his divine nature alone. Just as he is not partly divine and partly human, he is not partly holy. Jesus is holy in the entirety of his being—fully God and fully human. And as the measure of true humanity, Jesus is also the measure of what it means for humanity to be holy. This means that when one wants to know what human holiness looks like, one need look no further than the life of Jesus.

The life of Jesus is a great story, but it is so much more than just a heroic epic, even the greatest of all epics. In Jesus's life, we see the standard for human life. Jesus reveals in biographic form what it means to be holy. Jesus not only lived an exemplary moral life—one without sin (2 Cor. 5:21; Heb. 4:15; 1 Pet. 2:22)—but he also lived in full harmony with the will of God. He was fully obedient to what God wanted him to be and do. And he did so as a human.

Oftentimes in discussions regarding human holiness, the fullness and the authenticity of Jesus's humanity is downplayed, especially when we are considering the degree to which we will be held accountable to Jesus's example. We look for ways to excuse ourselves. We seek to shirk our responsibility by trying to distance Jesus's humanity from our own. We think that if we can just show that Jesus's humanity is unlike ours, we have shown that he is not really one of us. And if he is not one of us, then we cannot be held responsible to do what he has done. But in an attempt to let ourselves off the hook, we unwittingly turn to one ancient heresy or another. We may turn to Docetism, the view that Jesus only *appeared* to be human. This makes the incarnation into nothing more than an illusion. Or perhaps we turn to Apollinarianism, the view that Jesus was only *partly* human. We affirm that he had a physical human body. We may even grant that he displayed human emotions. Yet we assert that his mind and his will, those parts that make moral decisions, are not truly human but are instead wholly and only divine. This makes him significantly different from the rest of us. And since he is not like us, since he is more powerfully equipped than we are, we cannot be held to his standard. Such moves may ease our consciences, but they do not relieve us of our responsibilities. Since orthodox Christianity affirms Christ is *fully* human, we cannot escape being held to his example.[22]

Jesus is the example or standard of human holiness, but he is also the means by which humans are made holy. Throughout the history of the church, movements associated with holiness often believed that holiness could be attained through the exercise of discipline, dedication, and struggle. Holiness, it was believed, was within the grasp of each of us if we would simply knuckle down, work hard, and seize it. Yet, like so many contemporary fad diets, ultimately each of these pursuits resulted in a lot of frustration and failure but in little holiness. While earnestness and exertion are indispensable to the pursuit of holiness, on their own they are fundamentally inadequate.

Rather than being achieved through human effort and desire alone, the attainment of human holiness is dependent on the power of Christ. This power is not an abstract, impersonal force injected into humanity, enabling it to function in a way beyond what is natural. The power that brings about human holiness is not "something" but rather "Someone." Human holiness is attained by the indwelling and manifestation of the life of Christ, the Holy One. The holiness of humanity is nothing other than the holiness of Christ himself. Through the believer's intimate union with Christ, the holiness of the One who resides within infuses the one who hosts it. The holiness of a Christ-indwelt human being is not intrinsic to that human but is rather an imported, relational holiness.

Yet the Holy One who indwells humans also calls on them to join him in the process of their sanctification. The work that results in human holiness is a synergistic or cooperative work between Christ and those within whom he dwells. As stated earlier, human holiness is not solely the product of a rugged and determined individualism. Neither, however, is it quietism, an approach to the Christian life in which the human mind and body are completely inactive and one merely waits for God alone to act. In a quest for holiness, humans cannot be passive. We cannot sit idly back and falsely assume that since we cannot achieve holiness on its own, there is no role for us to play at all. Human holiness is the product of both the Holy One who dwells within and the cooperative striving and determination of the one in whom Christ so graciously dwells. Christian holiness is attainable only by the engagement of the believer and the cultivation and expression of the indwelling Christ by the power of the Spirit.

Defining Holiness

This quick survey of the understandings of holiness in the ancient Near East, the Old Testament, the Greco-Roman era, first-century Judaism, and the New Testament must lead us to reconsider a definition of holiness that places too much emphasis on behavior. Instead, as the term is used in this book, holiness is defined as *the transcendence or absolute otherness that is basic to God's being.* As we will see in the next chapter, this idea of transcendence or absolute otherness is not a purely negative category but is fundamentally connected to our understanding of God's being, including his moral perfection and other divine attributes. Strictly speaking, then, holiness is a property that is exclusive to God. Nothing else is intrinsically holy. Yet, in a relational sense, other things may legitimately be called "holy." This secondary sense of holiness is not intrinsic but is always and only derived from and dependent on an ongoing relation to God.

EXCURSUS: **Scripture's Role in Defining Holiness**

The Role and Limits of Intuition

Like so many other things, holiness is something we believe we can easily identify when we see it. We all believe we could identify holy people. Names like Mother Teresa, Mohandas (Mahatma) Gandhi, the Dalai Lama, and Billy Graham immediately come to mind, along with individuals we know more intimately: our grandparents, our pastor or priest, maybe even one of our teachers. We identify these people as holy based on what we know of their character, their behavior, their lifestyle, and, perhaps most important, how they have invested their lives.

At the same time, if we were to closely examine our lists, we might notice that some people are there simply on the basis of popular opinion or personal intuition rather than clear and explicit criteria of what constitutes holiness. If pressed, most of us would be unable to provide a clear and explicit rationale for why we named the ones we did. Very few of us would have matching lists, and we might even argue over whether certain individuals qualify for inclusion on the lists. Our intuitions might differ dramatically from one person to another.

In other words, even though we think we can identify holiness with some level of confidence when we see it, we lack a shared understanding or definition of the term. One is reminded (somewhat ironically) of the famous predicament in which the United States Supreme Court found itself in 1964 regarding what constituted hard-core pornography. In speaking for the concurring opinion, Associate Justice Potter Stewart famously declared: "I shall not today attempt further to define the kinds of materials I understand to be embraced within that shorthand description and perhaps I could never succeed in intelligibly doing so. But I know it when I see it."[23] Whatever may be the case for pornography, when it comes to holiness the difficulty lies in the fact that not all of us recognize it in the same instances as do others.

The lack of agreement regarding what holiness is and where it may be found is not an issue that exists solely between various religions. Different and sometimes even contradictory opinions on what holiness is and where it might be found exist within Christian circles. For example, Roman Catholicism has conferred on many the designation "saints" (holy ones), while many Protestant denominations resist the term "saints" even when they grant the relative goodness of certain people and their deeds. Even within Protestantism, and evangelical Protestantism in particular, there is disagreement on the definition of holiness and where examples of it might be found. There is no single evangelical definition or identification of holiness. This lack of agreement occurs even within denominations and, indeed, within their individual congregations.

Given this wide disagreement, the development of a helpful definition of holiness must go beyond both personal and corporate intuitions and gut feelings. If we are going to successfully pursue that which we say we desire and that which we need, and if we are going to be able to talk about it with any depth and precision, we will have to move beyond the leading of our intuitions.

The Role and Limits of Human Reason

One does not have to look very far to see the impressive results of the power of human imagination and its partner, human reason. A few years ago I was chatting with my wife's grandfather (who was then approaching 104 years old!) about the breadth of change he had seen in his lifetime. So many things that are now commonplace were rare or even nonexistent when he was young: the proliferation and sophistication of the automobile, the colossal advances in telecommunication, the rapid progress from rudimentary powered flight to the exploration of the moon and beyond, the invention and progress in computing technology and our growing dependence on it for almost all phases of life, the seemingly miraculous advances in the area of medical science. It is impossible to overestimate the impact that these developments have had on our lives and how radically different our world would be without them.

Yet there is another, much darker side to the potential of human imagination and reason that was also displayed throughout this same time period. While the twentieth century ushered in many great benefits for which we have human ingenuity to thank, it was also a time during which we witnessed how misdirected and misapplied human reason could be. It was a time that saw technology serve as the handmaiden of mass, inhumane destruction. Human reason discovered new ways to kill and destroy—and to do so on a scale unimaginable just a century prior. It was a century of war, genocide, torture, greed, and poverty, the scale of which was made possible by the imaginings and the inventions of human reason. And even when it is not taken in such a diabolical direction, human reason is neither infallible nor properly self-suspicious.

The Christian view of human reason is decidedly mixed. The Christian faith teaches that after the fall humanity became something less than it was created to be. Sin has caused humanity to become a twisted and misdirected being. Unfortunately, the maligning effects of sin are not limited solely to certain aspects of humans but include them all—not least the human ability to reason. Theologians call this maligning of human reason by sin the *noetic* effect of the fall.[24] (The term "noetic" comes from *nous*, the Greek word for "mind.") Due to the noetic effect of the fall, human reason cannot be wholly trusted. This may be especially true when it comes to considering spiritual issues, such as how to define and pursue holiness. Theologian John Webster has said that human reason, like the rest of the human condition, "is enclosed within the history of sin and reconciliation."[25] It too is fallen and therefore in need of redemption. It is bent and needs to be restored. In the words of the old hymn "Come, Thou Fount," the human intellect, like the human heart, is "prone to wander."[26]

In addition to its fallen condition, humanity is subject to the limits inherent to creatureliness. This means that the human ability to reason is just that—only human. There is only so much that it can do. It is not omniscient. While it has the ability to acquire and retain a vast array of knowledge—especially in cooperation with others—human reason (both individually and corporately) does not have the ability to see and to gather all the information associated with any particular issue. Therefore, humans must hold all the opinions gained from the exercise of reason tentatively and yield to and rely on forms of knowledge that are more certain and secure.

The Corrective Role of Scripture

Given the limitations of human intuition and reason that result from human creatureliness and fallenness, our definition of holiness must be derived not from intuition or reason but from Scripture—the divinely inspired witness of God and the church to the working out of God's plan of salvation in Jesus Christ. Scripture stands as both an authoritative corrective to and the standard for human understanding of the world of which it is a part. For the Christian, reliance on Scripture is indispensable to the pursuit of holiness. It defines clearly that which is otherwise vague.

Those pursuing holiness must respond to Scripture both because it is the self-communication of the Triune God and because it speaks clearly and authoritatively to the question of holiness (among other things). Scripture is *purposive*. Its raison d'être, reason for being, is not solely that of God's self-display but also to work toward human redemption. It seeks to overcome all that separates us from God—especially within ourselves—and to replace it with that which enables deep relationship with and conformity to God. Scripture's purpose is not merely propositional, not merely the conveying of information. While it certainly does such, its purpose is more than merely communication. Its purpose is transformation. Scripture should transform humanity cognitively, relationally, and morally. It should not merely tell us about holiness but should make us holy as well.

3

A Theological Investigation
of Holiness

Sometimes a movie's most memorable characters are not its most central. The often outlandish supporting characters, even those who appear only for a few moments and then are gone, lodge themselves deeply into audience members' memories. Such is the case in the 2003 blockbuster *Finding Nemo*.[1] In addition to lead character Nemo, the movie is full of other hard-to-forget characters: Nemo's addle-minded friend Dory, who was so memorable that she has become the lead character of a sequel; the surfer-talking turtle Crush; the dock-smart pelican Nigel; the trio of sharks-in-recovery, Bruce, Chum, and Anchor. And who can forget the flock of seagulls? They are not as endearing as Dory, as cool as Crush, or as daring as Nigel. And they don't deliver the same memorable line that the sharks do: "Fish are friends, not food!" They have but one line—or rather one *word*—that they repeat over and over and over again in a cacophony of confusion: "Mine!" And that which they claim as "Mine!" is not even theirs at all. Rather, it is something that they happen upon and wish, indiscriminately, to seize.

The current human situation is not all that different from the gulls. In its concupiscence[2]—the overwhelming, thoroughgoing, incessant desire for self-gratification—fallen humans are driven by a seemingly insatiable appetite to claim for themselves whatever they can lay their hands on (and maybe even that which is beyond their grasp). While this desire is often directed to material objects, it is not limited to such. In addition to an inordinate desire for "stuff," humans can also show an unhealthy and misdirected longing for less tangible things such as fame, significance, and love. In some Christian circles, this longing is even directed toward holiness. While we certainly should seek after holiness, our pursuit of it can easily become misdirected when we think of it as a commodity we can pursue and possess. Holiness is not a commodity, a *something*. Rather, as we saw in the last chapter, it is an attribute of God that is only derivatively attributed to anything else.

In the last chapter we briefly surveyed the ways in which holiness was understood in biblical times. In the Old Testament, the attribution of holiness to God is pervasive. Indeed, the single most-used adjective for God in the Old Testament is the word "holy" or one of its derivatives.[3] Likewise, the New Testament repeatedly refers to God's holiness and does so within the same basic categories of the Old Testament, namely, of transcendence, uniqueness, and being set apart from the mundane.

In this chapter I want to expand the understanding of holiness by looking more closely at God's attributes and their relation to holiness. When Scripture uses the word "holy" in relation to God, it does not impose an abstract category or definition of holiness to which God must conform. Rather, it presents us with a portrait of God and allows us to derive our understanding of holiness from that picture of God, "the Holy One of Israel." God is himself the very definition of holiness, the very standard of what it is to be holy.[4] Moreover, God is the source for all holiness, wherever it may appear. Nothing apart from God is intrinsically holy in the way that God is. If we are to expand our understanding of holiness, then, we must look closer at the nature and character of God.

Two Facets of Holiness

Today when the word "holiness" is used, often both the speaker and hearer attach to it a single idea: the strict and complete observation of one moral code or another. The association of holiness with morality and ethics has so captivated our minds that it can be difficult for us to imagine any other meaning of the word. Many of us simply assume the equation of holiness with moral perfection. Yet in Scripture holiness is not primarily about morality and ethics but about transcendence and otherness. Nevertheless, it would be an overcorrection to break the association between holiness and morality completely. Instead, in this chapter I argue that morality does have a proper role in how we understand holiness, but it is a subordinate role. Scripturally speaking, holiness first describes God's very mode of *being* and only secondarily his way of *behaving*.[5]

Holiness as Transcendence

At its very foundation, holiness refers to God's absolute uniqueness, his lack of peer or rival, his wholly otherness, or what we might call his "absolute categorical distinction." To talk about God in this way is to talk about his *transcendence*.

Understanding God's holiness to be rooted in his transcendence is clearly linked to the ancient Near Eastern understanding of holiness we observed in the previous chapter, the idea of holiness as that which is extraordinary. Yet the Christian understanding of holiness differs from the ancient Near Eastern one in at least one crucial way. In Scripture, the holy is not a realm or a category occupied by various entities that share similar characteristics but is rather a designation that is proper to God alone. In Scripture there is no understanding of the holy abstracted from the Holy One of Israel. There are no other gods but only those who would falsely and futilely masquerade as such. There is only one God, and therefore God is rightly described as holy because nothing else is like him.

Yet to say that God is holy is not merely to say what he is *not*; it is to affirm what he *is*. God's transcendence is not merely his otherness or his absolute categorical distinction from everything else. God manifests his otherness in particular ways, two of which I discuss below: aseity and Trinity.

The word "aseity" is derived from the Latin terms for "from" (*a*) and "self" (*se*). By attributing aseity to God, we declare that God owes his existence to no one and nothing other than himself. God is not dependent on anything for existence. He is uncaused, self-subsisting, and self-sufficient.[6] Clearly aseity is characteristic of God alone. According to the Christian faith, everything else that exists (no matter how old it may appear to be, no matter how grand it may seem) owes its origin and its ongoing existence to something beyond itself. In other words, everything else exists *contingently*. In contrast, God neither needs nor owes any other for his life.[7]

In the Old Testament, the very name of God, YHWH (Yahweh), declares his aseity. God has revealed his name to be "I

Am (that I Am)" (see Exod. 3:13–15). His name communicates that his existence is not contingent; it is intrinsic to his character. He just is. God is Being ("I Am").[8] Existence is basic to him. In a context where one's name so often identified one's descent from another—for example, Simon bar Jonah (Simon, son of Jonah)—and where one's genealogy was to some degree one's résumé, the fact that God's name fails to denote where he came from speaks volumes. God is without ancestry; God is without cause. He is the one who was, and is, and is to be (see Rev. 1:8; 4:8).

It may be that in his aseity God's transcendence, his holiness, is most clearly seen. God is the only one who owes his existence to no other. His holiness itself can be understood to be "of itself," to possess aseity. God's holiness does not have to measure up to a standard beyond itself but rather is the universal standard by which all others are measured.[9] God is not holy because he fulfills the requirements of some measure external to himself; he is himself the standard.

Not only in his aseity but also in his triune nature, God is wholly other. God alone exists as one substance in three persons. While various analogies to the Trinity have been offered as pedagogical devices—the three parts of an egg, the three forms of water, and so on—these analogies ultimately break down as explanations for the Trinity. Each illustrates some aspect of God's triune nature, but each is inadequate and at times even misleading. One might express God's unity at the expense of his plurality, while the other expresses God's plurality at the expense of his unity. No analogy accurately and fully reflects both the unity and plurality of God's nature, because nothing else shares God's triune nature. God alone is triune.[10]

Since holiness is an intrinsic property of God's nature, each person of the Godhead—Father, Son, and Holy Spirit—is holy, one no more than the other.[11] The Son and the Spirit are as holy as the Father. Holiness is not the property of one or another alone but is essentially and wholly proper to all three. There is not a tier of holiness within the Trinity.

In God's aseity and triune nature, God fulfills the ancient Near Eastern understanding of holiness as distinct from what is normal or beyond what is ordinary. Yet God's transcendence surpasses the ancient Near Eastern understanding of holiness by being extraordinary and absolutely unique. In God's aseity and triunity, God is not merely one member of a larger category of extraordinary beings; he is in a class all of his own. Scripture repeatedly testifies to the singularity of God:

> Who among the gods
>> is like you, LORD?
> Who is like you—
>> majestic in holiness,
> awesome in glory,
>> working wonders?
>> (Exod. 15:11)

> There is no one holy like the Lord;
> there is no one besides you;
> there is no Rock like our God.
>> (1 Sam. 2:2)

> Among the gods there is none like you, Lord;
>> no deeds can compare with yours.
>> (Ps. 86:8)

> This is what the LORD says—
>> Israel's King and Redeemer, the LORD Almighty:

> I am the first and I am the last;
>> apart from me there is no God.
>>> (Isa. 44:6)

> No one is like you, LORD;
>> you are great,
>> and your name is mighty in power.
>>> (Jer. 10:6)

Scripture is clear in its affirmation of God's transcendence, otherness, uniqueness, singularity. "Besides him there is no other" (Deut. 4:35).

Holiness as Moral Perfection

The secondary aspect of God's holiness is his unsurpassed and unsurpassable moral perfection. While I have argued that moral perfection is neither the sole nor even the primary meaning of the word "holiness," I do not deny that God's holiness includes his unsurpassed righteousness, even his moral perfection. When we confess the holiness of God, we affirm that God is righteous in all he does and says (Pss. 7:11; 50:6). Furthermore, we affirm that even his motives are always and only honorable. God always intends what is right, does what is right, and acts only for the best reasons.[12]

The problem with our typical understanding of holiness, then, is not that it includes this latter aspect but that it is often restricted to it. Moral perfection is indeed an essential aspect of God's holiness, but as we have seen, it does not exhaust the entirety of what the word "holiness" means. To limit holiness to the moral aspect alone is to attribute to it less than Scripture does. Such a narrow view fundamentally misunderstands the nature of holiness and, more important, the person of God himself. In order to further broaden our understanding of holiness, then, we turn to a consideration of its relation to a number of God's other attributes.

Holiness and the Attributes of God

Holiness is a characteristic of each person of the Trinity; it is also an aspect of each one of God's attributes. Theologians use the word "attribute" to mean something like an inherent characteristic, property, or quality of something. In the case of God, an attribute is not merely a characteristic that he possesses but, as Colin Gunton observes, it is something that God has revealed himself to be.[13] The number of attributes that could be ascribed to God is considerable,[14] but here I discuss only five—grandeur, personality, freedom, love, and eternality—paying particular attention to how the definition of each shapes our understanding of God's holiness and is shaped by what we understand God's holiness to be.

Grandeur

As mentioned earlier, I have always found the description of the divine throne room in Isaiah 6 to be particularly awe-inspiring. Isaiah paints a vivid picture of God's presence overwhelming the temple and shaking it to its very foundation. Through this portrait Isaiah seeks to communicate God's unmatched magnificence, the unparalleled power of his person, his unequaled grandeur. In the same scene, the seraphim, the attendants of the heavenly court, declare, "Holy, holy, holy is the Lord Almighty" (Isa. 6:3). This threefold declaration of God's holiness communicates its exhaustiveness, fullness, perfection, and unmatched grandeur.[15] Having been confronted with the utter grandeur and holiness of God, Isaiah immediately realizes his own unworthiness to be in God's presence or to be his suitable messenger (Isa. 6:5).

We can see God's grandeur revealed in his aseity, in God's total and absolute self-sufficiency. What could possibly be grander than to owe one's existence to no one or nothing other than oneself? In his grandeur, God is transcendent; he is unique; he is unmatched; he is holy.

Personality

When theologians state that God is "personal," they are not suggesting that he bears certain attractive social traits—that God is a "nice guy" or a "rather pleasant chap." Rather, when we speak of God as personal, we declare that he is capable of encountering others as subjects: speaking to them, listening to them, getting acquainted with them, becoming intimately involved with them.[16] Unlike the rest of us, God is not dependent on anyone else for personal relationship. God not only possessed personality prior to his work of creation, but he also exercised it. He did so within his own triune nature of Father, Son, and Holy Spirit. Jesus explicitly referred to the relationship that he shared with the Father prior to creation (John 17:5, 24). Indeed, it is in this eternal relationship among the Father, Son, and Holy Spirit that the personality of God finds its most intimate expression. Jesus holds up this eternal relationship as the model for the relations that his people are to have with him and with one another (John 17:11, 21). In this attribute, God's transcendence is once again evident. Other personal beings are able to enter into intimate relationship with another, but only God is able to fully express personality within God's own triune life—apart from interaction with any other being.

In his personality, God is transcendent; he is unique; he is unmatched; he is holy.

Freedom

God is not only personal; he is also free. When we speak of God's attribute of freedom, we declare that nothing constrains him. God is neither restricted by any outside force nor limited by any internal inadequacy. As humans, we all know what it is to be constrained. We are constantly limited both internally by the restrictions of our human nature and externally by forces beyond ourselves. In one way or another, all of our actions are limited by our physicality, the actions of others, and the resources (or lack thereof) available to us. In contrast, God's freedom means that he is unreservedly self-determined.[17] He can do whatever he wants to do, and he can do it exactly in the way he so desires. He is limited neither by his abilities nor by the resources at hand. In his freedom, God is not only *permitted* but also *able* to do whatever he likes. God's freedom is an expression of his holiness. He alone is truly and unreservedly free. He alone is unconstrained in doing as he desires.[18] In his freedom, God is transcendent; he is unique; he is unmatched; he is holy.

Love

The Christian definition of love is shaped by God's holiness. In common usage, the word "love" is something that may be directed in all sorts of ways to a variety of ends. Among these, the word "love" is often employed to describe two self-centered attitudes. First, "love" is used to identify narcissism, the adoration of the self to the exclusion of others: "self-love." Second, "love" may be employed to describe the act of using another for one's own pleasure or sexual self-gratification: a diminished view of what "making love" really means.

Divine love, however, stands firmly against such self-absorbed and self-serving attitudes and understandings. The kind of love God displays is expressed by the Greek word *agape*, a love that is neither self-centered nor self-serving but is instead primarily characterized by self-denial and self-sacrifice. As Jesus taught, such love is epitomized in the act of laying down one's life for one's friends (John 15:13). This kind of love is characterized by the laying aside of one's own desires, interests, and rights in favor of the other. It is characterized by submitting one's rights and prerogatives to the needs of the other for the advantage of the other. The epitome of this kind of love is seen in the incarnation, life, and death of Jesus Christ, who gave "his life as a ransom for many" (Mark 10:45; see also Matt. 20:28; 1 Tim. 2:6). Given the personal disinterest in this kind of love, it is not surprising that it is both unmerited and unchanging. This kind of love—the love of God expressed in the person and work of Jesus Christ—stands in stark contrast to the common, contemporary understandings of love mentioned above.

Scripture teaches us that God *is* love (1 John 4:8, 16). For God, love is neither merely an action that he may or may not perform nor merely an attitude that he may or may not have. Rather, in his very essence, God is love. Love is God's character. Consequently, all of his actions are based on love; God does nothing that is unloving. Even God's actions that display his justice or wrath are always loving. Even if we grant that humans can act in loving and disinterested ways at times (thus manifesting *agape*), not one of us acts this way all the time and without exception. It cannot be said of any one of us that we *are* love. We may at times act lovingly, but not one of us bears love as an essential attribute of our being. God, on the contrary, always acts in this way and does so without fail. God does not just love; he loves in the highest way, and he constantly does so. In his love, God is transcendent; he is unique; he is unmatched; he is holy.

Eternality

Finally, God is eternal. When we speak about the eternality of God, we affirm not only that God is everlasting but even more so that God's being is also not confined to space or time.[19] He is present to all things, in all places, and at all times. While eternality includes the idea that God has neither a beginning nor an end, it goes even further to include the idea that God is not captive to space and time at all. Space and time are inadequate categories for thinking of God. Space and time are not eternal but are themselves part of God's creation. Understandably, it is very hard for us to think of anything existing "outside" or "beyond" space and time, since our own lives and everything else we know, experience, or can even imagine are subject to both space and time.

Indeed, as parts of God's creation, space and time are subject to him; he is not subject to them. While he may act within them and use them for his purposes, he is not by nature confined by them. When we speak about God's eternality, we do not mean that God is immeasurably big or exceedingly ancient. Instead, we affirm that God's being is of such a different kind than the rest of creation that his existence defies the categories and control of space and time.[20] Nothing in all of creation exists in this way. Everything else in existence is in some way subject to time and space. Therefore, when we declare that God is eternal, we once again affirm God's holiness. In his eternality, God is transcendent; he is unique; he is unmatched; he is holy.[21]

Holiness—Just Another Attribute?

The question that naturally arises from a discussion of God's attributes is whether holiness is just another attribute of God like all of the others or whether it is in some way unique. Many theologians opt to identify holiness as simply one attribute among the others, which—needless to say—puts holiness in good company.[22] And if we define an "attribute" as simply an adjective one ascribes to God, then it is fair to say that holiness is an attribute like all the others. Clearly, as with the attributes discussed above, the word "holiness" identifies and describes God. Yet, while it can be helpful to describe each of God's attributes separately, as we have done above, one must be careful not to view them as discrete or distinct "components" of God, which together form the person of God. God is not a compilation or conglomeration of distinct components that come together to construct a being that we call "God." He is not some kind of divine Frankenstein's monster. Rather, each of the attributes can be understood only in their interrelation with the others, as collectively they describe the one, unified being of God.

There is thus a sense in which holiness—perhaps even in a way greater than some of the other attributes—is more than an attribute or predicate of God. While the term "holiness" undoubtedly describes the person of God, it also helps us to understand each and all of the attributes of God. Properly speaking, God is not merely a personal God, a free God, and a loving God; he is a God of *holy personality*, a God of *holy freedom*, and a God of *holy love*. Each and every attribute of God displays his holiness. We might say that holiness is an attribute of God as well as an attribute of each and every divine attribute. Rather than being an isolated aspect of his being, holiness thoroughly permeates the entirety of God's being. None of the other divine attributes can be properly understood apart from holiness.

From Divine Holiness to Human Holiness

The holiness of God fits both senses of the word that we described at the beginning of this chapter: he is both transcendent from all else that exists and morally perfect. Indeed, since God alone is truly transcendent (without peer or rival, the creator of all else), it may be said that God alone is holy. Yet one does not have to read very far into the Scriptures to find numerous other things deemed to be "holy": Judah is referred to as the "holy land" (Zech. 2:12); the church is described as a "holy people" (1 Cor. 1:2; Col. 3:12); the law of God is called "holy" (Rom. 7:12); and, most striking, the place in the temple where the presence of God was understood to be particularly present is called "the Most Holy Place" (Exod. 26:34; Heb. 9:3). Such biblical descriptions must be taken into account for a holistic theological understanding of holiness, and they might at first blush pose a problem for my definition of holiness, which is properly ascribable to God alone. However, I would argue that, in contrast to the holiness of God, the holiness of these other things, including humans, is not intrinsic to their nature. On their own, they are basely common. They are ḥōl. The people who make up the church are ordinary people. The soil that makes up the land of Palestine is nothing special. The words used to express the law are the same words that are used in other very common, perhaps even profane ways. Even the place that

Scripture refers to as "the holy of holies" or "the most holy place" is not special in itself; on its own it is just another room in just another building. The holiness of such things, things that Scripture declares to be holy, is not self-constituted. Rather, the holiness of such things is grounded in and flows from their relation to God. The holiness they possess is the result of being God's peculiar possession, of being set apart by him, of being used for his purposes, or of participating in his nature in some way. While it is proper to refer to such things as holy, it is essential to remember that their holiness is always a derived and alien holiness.[23]

The Holiness of the Incarnate Jesus

The relation between divine and human holiness is seen most intimately in the person of Jesus Christ. In Jesus, we have the one who is fully divine and therefore intrinsically holy. He is the one the Nicene Creed describes as "the only-begotten Son of God, begotten from the Father before all time, Light from Light, true God from true God, begotten not created, of the same essence as the Father, through Whom all things came into being."[24] Yet Jesus is also fully human. The same creed later declares his full humanity when it says that he "was incarnate by . . . the Virgin Mary and became human."[25]

As the eternal divine Son, as the second person of the Trinity, as the one who is "in very nature God" (Phil. 2:6), as the one whom the Chalcedonian Creed describes as "perfect . . . in deity" and "the selfsame one [who] is actually God,"[26] Jesus is intrinsically holy. Holiness is essential to Jesus's divine nature. He is holy in both aspects of the term: transcendent (unique, without peer) and morally perfect. First, with regard to Jesus's transcendence, Scripture repeatedly identifies Jesus by terms that designate both his holiness and his divinity. His holiness and divinity are both implied in the designation the "Son of God" (e.g., Matt. 11:25–30; 1 Cor. 15:28; Heb. 1:1–3, 5, 8). According to Matthew 28:19, Jesus is spoken of in equality with and shares the same "name" with the Father and the Holy Spirit. Those who flocked to Jesus realized that there was something distinct about him, and they thus referred to him as God's "holy servant Jesus" (Acts 4:27, 30). Both his divinity and his holiness are implied in his own ability to make others holy (1 Cor. 1:2; 1 Thess. 3:13; Heb. 10:10). Even those fundamentally opposed to his ministry, the demons, recognized Jesus's divine nature and his essential holiness when they referred to him as "the Holy One of God" (Mark 1:24; Luke 4:34).

Yet, in addition to asserting that Jesus is "fully God," the Scriptures and historic Creeds of the church also declare his full humanity. In describing Jesus's humanity, the Chalcedonian Creed specifies that he is not just human but "of the same reality as we are ourselves" and "perfect . . . in [his] humanness."[27] He is neither *just* divine nor *just* human. Nor is he a mongrel, a mixture of some divinity and some humanity. Nor is he just a portion of humanity added to the fullness of divinity (or vice versa). He is *fully* God and *fully* human. This condition of being at one and the same time fully God and fully human in one person—called the "hypostatic union"—is found in no one else other than Jesus.[28]

Second, with respect to Jesus's moral perfection, Scripture again clearly denotes that Jesus, while fully human in nature, did not conform to the otherwise common or universal human practice of committing sin. This combination of Jesus being fully human and being without sin is made explicit by the author of the Epistle to the Hebrews and is essential to the point that he is trying to make. Hebrews explicitly states that Jesus is fully human in every way yet without sin (2:17; 4:15). The nature of Jesus's moral perfection is not limited to the passive or the negative; it does not rest solely on his *not* having broken God's law. Sin is not limited to doing something that one should not do (sins of commission); it is also sinful to leave undone those things that should be done (sins of omission). It is true that Jesus did not commit sin, and this means that he also did not fail to do that which is good and right. He was active and thorough in pursuing and achieving the call of God in his life; he did everything that God intended for him to do (Rom. 5:19). Moreover, he pursued this even when it was difficult and costly to do so (Phil. 2:8; Heb. 5:8).

Jesus as Our Example of Holiness

Each of us is prone to excuse our own shortcomings, to vindicate our personal faults. It seems to be human nature to do so. As far back as the garden of Eden, humans have blamed others for their sins. Adam blamed his failure on both Eve and God, who gave her to him (Gen. 3:12). Today one of the ways that we continue to excuse our shortcomings is to distance Jesus from us. When confronted with the moral perfection of Jesus, we are quick to protest that he is not like us and that this difference is the secret to his impeccable behavior. Yet we must not assume that the sole reason for Jesus's sinlessness and his full conformity to the will of God is the power inherent in his divine nature. On multiple occasions, Scripture reminds us that the power for Jesus's life and ministry came not from his own divine nature but from being "full of the Holy Spirit" (Luke 4:1). Jesus himself identifies the indwelling Spirit as the source of his power for both life and ministry. The Spirit is identified as Jesus's power to resist temptation (Matt. 3–4; Luke 4–5),[29] to teach with authority (Luke 4:14–15; John 3:34), and to cast out demons (Matt. 12:28). Jesus's dependence on the Spirit does not deny his divine nature; it simply recognizes the natural limitations of his human nature that he fully assumed.[30]

Jesus's dependence on the Spirit can therefore serve as an encouragement to his followers rather than as a discouragement or an excuse to pursue and be satisfied with something less. As Keith Warrington notes, "The recognition that the Spirit partnered [with] Jesus at the beginning of his mission would be a constant encouragement to the early believers as they began their missions without his bodily presence. The Spirit who walked with [and empowered] Jesus would be united with them in their quest to preach the same good news as that presented in Jesus' first recorded sermon in Nazareth. Although their commissions were different from his, the Spirit would partner them with the same quality of support as he gave to Jesus."[31]

It should come as no surprise, therefore, that as remarkable as Jesus's ministry was in these areas, it was not unique. Scripture identifies others who performed similar feats. We could note the remarkable pioneering ministry of John the Baptist (Luke 1); the Pentecost sermon of Peter, which received a greater response than any sermon that Jesus ever preached (Acts 2); Stephen's stirring defense of the faith before the Jewish ruling council, the Sanhedrin (Acts 7); and the extraordinary missionary exploits of Paul and Barnabas (Acts 13). In each of these instances, Scripture explicitly identifies the power for these miraculous acts as the presence of the Holy Spirit.

This does not mean that we must deny or downplay Jesus's divine nature. Rather, it calls the church to an understanding of Jesus that affirms the reality of *both* his fully divine and his fully human natures. Too often we sacrifice the fullness of one to the supremacy of the other. When we are confronted with Jesus's impeccable behavior, we excuse our own shortcomings by denying that he was "really" human like we are. After all, we protest, he was *also* divine. If we give in to the common heresy of practically denying the full humanity of Jesus, however, we sabotage the entire Christian hope for salvation—for it is founded at least as much on Christ's humanity as his divinity—and we also deny his ministry as our pilgrim, our teacher, and our example. If he is not subject to the same temptations and limitations as the rest of humanity is, naturally his actions and attitudes cannot serve as authentic examples for us. An example is simply a lesson on how to move forward in the face of particular temptations and limitations. While we might learn something about Jesus from his own life, if he is not fully human, if he is not bound to the same natural limitations that we are, we cannot learn from him either how to live a holy life or what it means for humanity to please God. If he is not fully human, he cannot be—as Scripture describes him and as he described himself (John 13:15; 1 Cor. 11:1; 1 Tim. 1:16; 1 Pet. 2:21)—our example.

Conclusion

With transcendence at the heart of what holiness means and with God as the epitome of transcendence by his very nature, one might logically conclude that God's holiness would prohibit his relating with anything else and, particularly, with a humanity that is stained by sin. The good news is that the holiness of God is so transcendent that it even transcends an absolute transcendence! The nature of the holiness of God is such that in love it seeks the other. It is a holiness that seeks to bring others to itself rather than categorically rejecting everything else. It is a holiness that desires to make the other its own. It is what theologian John Webster has called a "fellowship-creating" holiness.[32]

In the following chapters, then, we build on our biblical and theological discussion of divine holiness to a fuller discussion of how holiness relates to God's purposes for humanity. We will continue to draw from revelation rather than intuition as our guiding light. As we will see, God's desire for relationship with humans is the very reason why he has shown himself to us. The purpose of divine revelation is for God to be in relationship with humanity. In spite of what may be popular opinion, the primary purpose of revelation is not the communication of information. Divine revelation in its various forms, including Scripture, does not have as its ultimate goal the mere changing of human minds and opinion. While it may certainly do such, the primary goal of God's self-revelation to humanity is to establish "a new *human* possibility"[33]—the transformation of humanity through a relationship with the divine. By revealing himself to humanity, God seeks to overcome that which bars humanity from communion with him. The goal of God's communication with humanity is to sanctify it, to make it holy. As Webster notes, the purpose of revelation is to overcome human opposition to him, its alienation from him, and its self-centered and self-sufficient pride.[34] Revelation seeks to replace these with a true knowledge of God, a love for God, and a sober but appropriate fear of God. By presenting himself to humanity, God seeks to establish fellowship, communion, and even union with humanity instead of seeking to drive humanity even further away from him. Therefore, to know God in the way that God intends for us to know him does not have its ultimate expression in merely learning something about God. Its greater purpose is human relational and moral transformation—and ultimately human glorification in the new heavens and new earth.

EXCURSUS: ## Human Language and the Nature of God

In this chapter we have discussed how God, who is the subject of theology proper, is holy. We saw how God's holiness signifies not only his moral perfection but also, and even more fundamentally, his absolute transcendence. Because of God's transcendence, human language is only an imperfect tool to describe God's nature. Human language developed to identify and to communicate humans' experience of life in the world. Words and phrases are created whenever humans experience something new and wish to identify and talk about it. Human language is thus fundamentally *earthly*.

Since God's nature transcends our earthly experience and is far more magnificent than anything in creation, it is beyond the descriptive ability of human language. It is not that our sincere and thoughtful attempts to speak about God are necessarily wrong but rather that human language is simply ill-equipped to describe God fully. Even when humans may speak of God *accurately*, we can never describe him *exhaustively*.

How then is humanity to speak about God? While recognizing the inadequacy of our best words to describe God, Christian theologians have developed two ways that we can speak of God without misrepresenting him. The first is called the *apophatic* approach. Since God's nature exceeds our ability to express it, this approach seeks to describe God in terms of *what God is not*.[35] Without even realizing it, we use such apophatic, or negative, language often when describing God. We take concepts and properties that we see in the world and note that God is not like them. So, for example, a familiar hymn includes two apophatic terms in its title: "Immortal, Invisible, God Only Wise." The terms "*im*mortal" and "*in*visible" are apophatic terms. They do not assert what God is but what he is not. Unlike most living creatures, God is neither mortal nor visible. Such apophatic language is necessary when talking about God since, as we have seen, God is so unlike the creation within which human language developed.

The second way that we speak about God is the *kataphatic* (sometimes *cataphatic*) approach, the attempt to make positive statements to describe *what God is*.[36] Fundamental to such an approach is the humble recognition that the language at our disposal is by its very nature inadequate to describe the fullness of God. Still, the kataphatic approach takes the inadequate language available to us and uses it to describe God as best we can. In some cases, the kataphatic approach takes those properties that we have observed in the world around us— things like power (potency), knowledge (science), and locality (presence)—and expands them to their supreme degree. We supercharge the words. Thus "power" becomes "omnipotence" (all-powerfulness), "knowledge" becomes "omniscience" (all-knowingness), and "locality" becomes "omnipresence" (ubiquity or pervasiveness). Rather than inventing new categories that speak directly of who God is, we take words that describe what we experience in creation and expand and refit them to refer to God's way of being.[37]

Given the limitations of human language, we must be careful to realize that even when we use kataphatic language, God's nature can still stretch and burst the natural capacity of our words. We must therefore always remember that the God we confess is beyond the capacity of human language to fully express. Indeed, even the best of our descriptions of God must be understood to be to a certain degree metaphorical or analogical. Instead of describing God precisely and completely, our language can say only what God is like or is not like. As a human invention, language draws on humans' experience of human life and surroundings. When humans try to describe God, we have no choice but to use these words, phrases, concepts, and categories we have developed. Yet because language is grounded on a creaturely experience of creation, the words, phrases, and categories we use are always inadequate to fully express who God is. This is not to say that such words, phrases, and categories are thoroughly powerless. It is rather to remind us that such descriptions are limited and that we must therefore use them with humility.[38]

4

Holiness and the Nature and Purpose of Humanity

I usually do not mind admitting that I am a child of the 1960s. It was a great time to be a kid! If you had visited my neighborhood back then, you would have found my friends and me running down the streets with towels pinned like capes to our backs as we pretended to be any of a variety of superheroes. While Batman was the most popular at the time, one of the other preferred roles was the Man of Steel, Superman. At the opening of the classic Superman television show, a crowd on the city street looks into the sky, as various people shout those memorable lines: "It's a bird!" "It's a plane!" "It's Superman!" Though they are all looking at the same thing, the crowd who observes this streaking figure against the sky does not agree about what it is that they see. Likewise, although we each encounter people every day, there exists a wide range of opinion about what it means to be human. In spite of our vast scientific knowledge about the species *Homo sapiens*, there exists a surprising variety of opinions, even within the church, concerning what it means to be human. In this chapter I describe some of these diverse opinions before offering a biblical and theological account of humans as created in the *imago dei*, the image of God. As we will see, this concept connects our understanding of humanity with our account of holiness offered in the previous chapters. Only when we have a proper understanding of humanity's nature and purpose can we know what it means for humans to be holy.

What Does It Mean to Be Human?

People from all sorts of academic disciplines have opinions concerning anthropology (the study of humanity) and what it means to be human. In the field of bioethics, for example, debates over issues regarding embryonic stem cells, abortion, cloning, and euthanasia often center on the question of what it means to be human. With the question of abortion, debates often turn to the question of when life begins,[1] but even this question presupposes an understanding of what it means to be human.[2] The question of whether abortion is a crime stands squarely on the question of what it means to be human: When does a fetus move from being just a collection of animated cells, a something, to becoming a person, a someone? This question is important because most people grant that there is a particular value to human life that is in some way higher than that of other life forms.

Likewise, in the field of biology there is little doubt that the investigation of the origin of our species has garnered attention well beyond the walls of the academy over the past 150 years. If there is one thing that Charles Darwin proved with the publication of his theory in *On the Origin of Species* in 1859,[3] it is that there is still no consensus on what it means to be human. Many understood Darwin's theory (or the other theories derived from it) to be a direct challenge to the accuracy and authority of the Scriptures. Yet more directly it seemed to challenge the church's long-held and deeply invested beliefs regarding the origin and nature of the human species.[4] Consequently, the discussion concerning human origins has sat center stage in theological anthropology for over a century. This is especially true in the area of Christian apologetics, where the threat was deemed serious enough to launch a full-scale assault on Darwin, his theory, and their ideological offspring.[5]

While the *where*, *when*, and *how* questions of human origins are important ones, I would argue that they are secondary to the *who*, *what*, and *why* questions: Who are we? Why do we exist? What are we to be and to do? Such existential questions of life are significantly more important and pressing for our day-to-day lives than is the question of how we got here.

After looking at the violence and the tragedy of life that surrounds us—wars, crime, gang violence, corporate greed, child abuse, mass shootings—one could easily conclude that humanity is inherently and inescapably evil. It is easy and almost natural to be pessimistic about the nature and destiny of humanity after watching the evening news. The social sciences seem to have nothing more encouraging to add. Pronouncements concerning human nature from sociologists and psychologists, for example, seem far from optimistic. Even the actor Johnny Depp (who is neither a psychologist nor a sociologist) succinctly expresses what many from these disciplines recognize: "We're all damaged in our own way. Nobody's perfect. I think we're all somewhat screwy, every single one of us."[6]

Scripture confirms this pessimistic analysis. It identifies the universal human condition as fallen, depraved, corrupt, wicked, and perverse (e.g., 2 Chron. 6:36; Ps. 5:9; Isa. 53:6; Jer. 17:9; Mark 7:21–23; Rom. 3:23; 7:18; Titus 1:15–16). What's more, the Christian tradition suggests that this condition is not localized or isolated to one particular area of the human but has instead infected all aspects of human being. This condition—one might call it a disease—is not limited to the will, the reason, or the libido; it includes every aspect of the human: the mind, the heart, the body, the spirit, and so on. No aspect of human nature, no matter how seemingly remote or isolated, has escaped unscathed. Some within the Christian tradition have called this human condition "totally depraved."[7]

The silver lining to this picture of the human condition is that what we now see in humanity in all of its tragedy, wretchedness, and "screwiness" is not the way it began or the way it was meant to be.[8] Despite its reputation for pessimism, the Christian view of humanity is a fundamentally positive one. Though the Christian tradition admits the universal depraved condition of humanity, it does not concede that this is the way things started out, that this is the way things ought to be or must be, or that this is the way things will be. Without denying that humanity is deeply troubled, the Christian faith asserts that the way humanity may be is neither the way it began nor the way it will remain.

According to the Christian tradition, the current condition of humanity is an abnormal condition. In other words, to be human is not necessarily to be the depraved creature—the scarred, grotesque, and even alien creature—that we currently experience.[9] Christianly speaking, true humanity is what came from the hand of God, unspoiled and untwisted, which is exemplified in the person of Jesus Christ and will inhabit the coming heavenly kingdom.[10] In short, the Christian tradition affirms that humanity is a *holy* creation, though what it exactly means by this will require some unpacking.

Human Holiness and the *Imago Dei*

The central biblical expression for describing humanity is that God made humanity in the *imago dei*, the image of God. This is the first thing that must be stated regarding human nature. Biblically speaking, in spite of all the human treachery that surrounds us, the image of God is the essence of human nature. The image of God distinguishes humanity from the rest of creation, as this expression is used in Genesis only in reference to humanity. Though all creation is created "good" (Gen. 1:4, 10, 12, 18, 21, 25) and together is even "very good" (Gen. 1:31), only humanity is created "in the image of God" (Gen. 1:26–27). Since the doctrine of the *imago dei* is central to a biblical understanding of human nature, it unavoidably shapes discussions of human holiness as well. In what follows, then, I offer a definition of the *imago dei* before discussing how this understanding of the *imago dei* relates to our understanding of holiness as presented in the previous chapters.

Defining the *Imago Dei*

Throughout its history, the church has seen a variety of opinions on what the *imago dei* is. Taking it in a crudely literal way, some have proposed that it means nothing more and nothing less than humanity looks like God. On this view, sometimes called the *substantive view*, God is a physical being, and when he made humanity, he made something that in some way physically resembles him.[11] Such a belief, however, has rightly been rejected by most Christians through the ages, since Scripture consistently teaches that God is spirit and, apart from the incarnation, spirit alone (John 4:24). The view that God has a physical body has been deemed to be heretical, and so whatever the *imago dei* means, it cannot mean this.

Others have argued that the *imago dei* is seen in functions that humanity was created to accomplish or fulfill, including God's call on humanity to rule or have dominion over the earth (Gen. 1:26–28). In this way, humans reflect on earth, even if only in a relative way, the sovereignty of God over his creation. According to this *functional view*, when humans express sovereignty over creation in the way God would, they most clearly display the *imago dei*.[12] Yet if the *imago dei* is dependent on a function that humans can choose to or not to perform, then it is a conditional rather than essential feature of human nature, which runs contrary to the teaching of Scripture.

A third view attempts to define the *imago dei* by taking into account not only the full testimony of Scripture but also the essential nature of God as triune. Known as the *relational view*, this belief holds that the *imago dei* is not something inherent to particular individuals but is something that describes humanity collectively and in relationship with one another and, most important, with God. From this perspective, it is more accurate to say that the relation itself, rather than any one of the individual members of that relationship, is the *imago dei*. The *imago dei* is grounded not in the ability of an individual to engage in relationships but in the dynamic relation itself that images God.[13] While the *imago dei* is innate to humanity in its particular relationship to God, it is most fully reflected when humans are united with Christ by the power of the Holy Spirit.

It is only then that humans are, as each person of the Trinity is and has always been, in intimate union with the divine.

According to this relational view of the *imago dei*, humanity can be God's image bearer in two senses: the formal sense and the material sense.[14] According to the formal sense, God has created humanity with capacities similar to those possessed by God, including the capacities to reason, to be responsible, and to be free. These capacities already distinguish humanity from the rest of creation to a degree. As long as humanity has these formal capacities, it reflects the divine nature formally. While fallen humanity's ability to reason, to be responsible, and to be free are limited and misdirected, the formal capacity for these actions remain. In this way, even a fallen human continues to possess and exercise the image of God. According to twentieth-century theologian Emil Brunner, a noted proponent of the relational view, the formal sense is the understanding of the *imago dei* described in the Old Testament.[15]

The material sense of the *imago dei* does not contradict the formal sense or the Old Testament testimony, but it does suggest that there is more to the image than just what is found in humanity's various capacities. According to the material sense, when God created humanity—part of that which he declared "very good"—his intentions for humanity were not complete. God's plan for humanity was to continue to work with this "very good" creature in order to make even more of it. In particular, by continuing to work with humanity after its creation, God was to bring humanity to a realization of and a responsibility for the capacities that were part of its formal *imago dei*.[16] God's intent was to take humanity, equipped with the capacities that are identified in the formal sense of the *imago dei*—will, reason, freedom—and to teach humans to utilize these abilities by responding, "Yes, I am Thine,"[17] to God in love and in freedom. When humans say yes to God, they employ these capacities in the same way God does. In the formal sense, the *imago dei* is simply the *possession* of these capacities; in the material sense, it is the *expression* of them in accordance with God's will. As the persons of the Trinity have eternally and without exception said, "Yes, I am Thine," to one another, the material expression of the *imago dei* in humans is to say yes to God as well. When humans were created, they possessed the *imago dei* formally, but as they are perfected, they express the *imago dei* materially. It is from the material form of the image that we get our current understanding of holiness as moral perfection. For the Christian faith, moral perfection is not fulfilling a long list of "dos" or avoiding an equally long list of "do nots." Ultimately, moral perfection is grounded in free and loving surrender to God's will and in intimate relationship with God. It is saying, "Yes, I am Thine."

Supporting this relational understanding of the *imago dei* is an interesting detail found in both Genesis 1:27 and 5:1–2. These passages state that humanity was made in the image of God and that in this image humanity was created male and female. In other words, that which is described as being created *imago dei* bears within it the intent of intimate relationship, not only with God but also with one another. In its very composition as male and female, humanity—as with the Trinity—has an internal and essential diversity and complementarity.

One of the practical weaknesses of popular understandings of the *imago dei* is the belief that the image can be possessed by humans quite independently of any active relation to the One whose image it is. Some seem to believe that the image of God is a property that can exist independent of God himself.[18]

The relational view of the *imago dei*, in its formal and material senses, clearly rejects this misunderstanding. The formal aspect was bestowed on humanity by the will and power of God. It was his idea to make humanity with these capacities, and it was his touch that made it so, as the Genesis creation account makes clear. The necessity of that relationship with God is even clearer with respect to the material aspect in which relationship with God is essential to the possibility of the moral perfection of humans. Furthermore, since both the formal and the material aspects of the image have been damaged by the fall, we are reminded that the image is not as resilient or independent as we might like to think. It is always and everywhere dependent on God for its continued existence. The image of God can never be disconnected from the God whose image it is.

The *Imago Dei* and Holiness as Transcendence

The Christian tradition affirms that there are only two categories of being in the universe: creator and creation. The first category is reserved for God alone.[19] The second category includes everything, besides God, that ever was, is, and will ever be.[20] In these terms, humanity is in the same category as everything else in creation. As such, humanity is pretty ordinary. As they would have said in the ancient Near East, humanity is *ḥōl*.

Yet this is not all that there is to say about humanity. While in one sense humanity is in the same category as the rest of creation, it is just as true that nothing else was created in the *imago dei*.[21] From this latter perspective, humanity's holiness can be seen in the way in which humanity was set apart from the rest of the created order. In Genesis 1, the rhythm of creation moves steadily along, day after day, until God announces that he is going to create humanity in his image. Rather than simply calling humanity into existence as he had in every creative act previously, he declares that he will make humans and that he will make them in his image (Gen. 1:26). He then creates the first human, blesses him, commissions him, and tells him how he has provided for him. With this event the rhythm of creation is interrupted. The creation of humanity, while remaining a part of the overall creation story, stands apart from the creation of everything else. The description of humanity's creation in Genesis 2 only reinforces the uniqueness of humanity's creation. In Genesis 1, the rest of creation, it seems, is simply summoned into being. In Genesis 2, however, humanity is the product of a much more intimate method. Unlike the rest of creation, the first human does not come into being solely in response to divine command; he is brought into existence and brought to life from the direct touch of God, who personally fashions him and breathes life into him (Gen. 2:7).[22]

The holiness of humanity extends beyond the method by which it was created. That humanity bears God's image marks its distinction and even transcendence from the rest of the creation. While the original act of creating humans in God's image is an event now long in the past, humanity's continued possession of the image remains. It may be tempting to assert that the image disappeared with the fall,[23] but the Christian tradition affirms that the image remains, even if it is marred, maligned, and diminished. That humanity continues to bear the image, even after the fall and in the face of ongoing sin, is seen in Genesis 9:6. There we find God's prohibition of murder. Rather than noting the many devastating social consequences of murder, God notes that the crime in murder is not simply that it is beyond the rights of one creature to take the life of another; the crime in murder is that it is an affront against the image of God that continues in some way to reside in humanity. Likewise, when James writes that "with the tongue we praise our Lord and Father, and with it we curse human beings, who have been made in God's likeness" (James 3:9), the power of his argument is lost if we fail to affirm that there *currently* exists a connection between God and the ones who were created in his image.[24] Similarly, theologian G. C. Berkouwer has observed that when Paul writes "a man ought not to cover his head, since he is the image and glory of God" (1 Cor. 11:7), this instruction "[makes] sense in the context only if applied to man as he is now, since the Fall."[25] In short, despite the devastating effects of the fall, humans are still distinct from the rest of creation as the sole bearers of the *imago dei* among all creatures. In this way, humanity is seen to be holy in the first and primary understanding of the term: transcendence.

The *Imago Dei* and Holiness as Moral Perfection

As we saw in the previous chapter, holiness can refer both to something's mode of existence (transcendence) and to the way that something acts (moral perfection). Having been created in God's image, humanity is holy in the sense of transcendence. The human is a different kind of being—one might even say a *higher* kind of being—than the rest of the creaturely world. Humans may be holy in the second sense too. As radical as it may sound, it is possible to be human and to be morally perfect— without spot, blemish, or ethical imperfection. It is possible for humans to do what is right and avoid what is wrong.[26] When it comes to humanity, this kind of holiness is certainly not essential to its being in the same way that being created in the *imago dei* is. Rather, it is conditional. It is subject to perversion, distortion, and corrosion, and some would suggest even annihilation. This is especially true in beings that possess a level of God-given self-determination. Ironically, the *imago dei* may even play a role in its own deterioration: if to be created in the image of God means that humans possess free will, then the mishandling of that free will could result in sin and thereby in a tarnishing of the *imago dei*. Nevertheless, as we saw in the case of the fully human Jesus, holiness as moral perfection is not contrary to human nature, even if it is not currently the norm.

Jesus—the Archetype of Humanity

When discussing theological anthropology in my courses, I often raise the question of who serves as the archetypal human. More often than I care to admit, students will propose that we look to the pre-fall Adam for our example of what it means to be authentically and fully human. After all, they propose, Adam was sinless and occupied with nothing but his relationship with God and the work God had given to him. What more would we expect? But given what I've argued in this chapter about the relationship between the *imago dei* and holiness, I hope that it is clear why this answer misses the mark. When we look for the human archetype—for the ideal (and not just the first) example of what it means to be human—we must not turn to the pre-fall Adam. Adam was part of that which was created "very good," was in communion with God, and was occupied with the work that God had given to him, but he was not yet perfected. He was not everything that God intended for humans to be. He bore an unspoiled formal image of God, but he did not yet exhibit that image materially in all the ways that God intended. As discussed in this chapter's excursus below, human perfection is far more than just innocence. The goal of human perfection is full and perfect communion with God and his creation. As Paul wrote to the Corinthians, we should look not to Adam as our model but to the second Adam, Jesus Christ (1 Cor. 15:45–49). Jesus serves as the perfect example of what it means to be human. The Christian need look no further than to Jesus as the human archetype.

To take Christ as the archetype of humanity requires a commitment to reject the heresies discussed in chapters 2 and 3. As we saw in those chapters, the historic, orthodox view is that in the incarnation Jesus not only reveals God to humanity; he also reveals *humanity* to humanity. In Jesus Christ, we see not only who God is but also what it means to be truly human. He shows us what we are to be like. Instead of being the exception, he serves as the epitome of human being in all of its various aspects—its actions, motivations, priorities, and so on.[27] Jesus reveals to us the goal of the material *imago dei*, and in so doing he reveals what it means for humans to be holy.

Conclusion

Every day we see evidence that could lead us to conclude that holiness and humanity have little in common. We may be tempted to despair that holiness is out of reach for fallen humans. However, as we have seen in this chapter, holiness is a fundamental aspect of humanity as made in the *imago dei*. As creatures made in the image of God, humans—in a relative but still real way—transcend the rest of creation, thus reflecting God's holiness formally. Moreover, humans are invited to participate in the divine nature through union with Christ, thus reflecting God's holiness materially. Yet, as we will discuss further in the following chapters, humanity has fallen into sin and thus diminished the image of God. Eminent playwright George Bernard Shaw once observed that "only on paper has humanity yet achieved glory, beauty, truth, knowledge, virtue, and abiding love."[28] While Shaw's pessimism may be warranted, Scripture teaches us that holiness is more than just a hypothetical possibility for humanity. It has been achieved in the fully human Jesus Christ, who invites us to participate with him in the holiness of God. As we will see, the salvation he brings is not merely deliverance from sin but is a transformation of the human more and more into the image of God. Moreover, this transformation takes place not only in various individuals but within the church, the body of Christ.

EXCURSUS: **Moral Perfection, Human Innocence, and Human Limitations**

When used in the context of discussions of human holiness, the term "moral perfection" can easily cause confusion or misunderstanding. Before concluding our discussion of human nature and turning to a discussion of the problem of sin, then, it may help to unpack what "moral perfection" does and does not mean when used in these contexts. In particular, I want to clarify the relation of moral perfection to two related but distinct concepts: human innocence and human limitations.

Moral Perfection and Human Innocence

Scripture teaches that humanity was created in innocence. In the beginning, humanity was free from the experience and the taint of sin and guilt. Humanity was free to relate intimately with others and with God. This innocence was short-lived,[29] but it nevertheless indicates that there was a time during which humanity did not sin. While it may currently be the universal human experience, it is not essential to what it means to be human.

Many assume that the term "innocence," when applied to this original state of sinlessness, is relatively synonymous with the term "moral perfection," but moral perfection implies far more than mere innocence. The word "perfection" carries at least two related though distinct definitions. On the one hand, the term "perfect" can mean without qualification, absolute, or to an ultimate degree. On the other hand, "perfect" can also mean "having all the essential elements, qualities, or character-istics."[30] The first definition of "perfect" restricts its proper use to God alone. God alone is absolute. Everything else that exists has limitations and constraints. In philosophical theology, this first understanding of perfection has even been used to define God and to attempt to prove his existence. Anselm (1033–1109 CE), a theologian and archbishop of Canterbury, argues in what has been called the "ontological argument" for the existence of God that God is "that than which nothing greater can be conceived"[31]—in order words, that God is absolute perfection.

The second definition of "perfect" is relative to the nature of the thing described. It does not indicate that the thing is absolutely perfect in all possible ways; rather, it indicates that something fulfills all the characteristics essential to its nature. In this sense, we can talk about the "perfect" chair, for example. A chair is perfect when it fulfills both the form and the function of what we understand "chairness" to be. It need not be more than a chair, but it cannot lack that which is essential to being a chair.

As argued earlier in this chapter, the humanity that we see prior to the fall was not everything God intended for it to be. It was innocent, but it was not perfect. Scripture indicates that humanity, while created good and innocent, had a purpose greater than simply to maintain that state of innocence. Humanity was created to be in the image of God, both formally and materially. Exhibiting the image of God cannot mean less than to love, since God is love (1 John 4:8). On the one hand, this love for God and for others is to be *processive*—active, dynamic, actual rather than just potential. On the other hand, it is to be *progressive*—growing, expanding, maturing (Eph. 4:15; Phil. 1:9; 1 Thess. 3:12; 4:1, 19; 2 Thess. 1:3). As the Westminster Shorter Catechism states, humanity's "chief end" is "to glorify God, and to enjoy him forever."[32] While this may have begun in the garden of Eden, its complete expression was not fully realized there. The relationship between humanity and God of which the Catechism speaks is a dynamic, ongoing relationship.

Since God is essentially and eternally triune—in relation among Father, Son, and Spirit—those who reflect God's image must also reflect this relational aspect. All humans are *related* to God as creature to creator, but our end is more than that: it is to be in *relationship* with him.[33] This relationship can be neither shallow nor conventional. Reflecting the nature of the Triune God, it is to be intimate and deep—we in him and he in us. This can happen only as humans are indwelt by the Spirit of God (John 14:20; 1 John 3:24; 4:13). So deep and thorough is the relationship we are to have with him that it may be truly said that, in so doing, we "may participate in the divine nature" (2 Pet. 1:4). Only then can we truly say that we have been perfected.

Moral Perfection and Human Limitations

To participate in the divine nature is to be holy, but it is not to overcome the limitations inherent to humanity. While participating in the divine nature cannot help but lift humans to a higher plane of existence, it does not make humans into the divine.[34] While such participation may be rightly termed "divinization," such divinization is always and constantly dependent on God; it is never a natural or essential characteristic of humanity.[35] It is received by grace and maintained by grace. Even when participating in the divine nature, humans remains human.[36] Even while humans participate in the divine nature, they maintain the appropriate and "good" creaturely limitations. Humans remain physical beings with all the limitations inherent to physicality, including limits with respect to knowledge. Such limitations are not bad. Even Jesus experienced the limitations of physicality and knowledge during his time on earth. He became tired and hungry. He learned new things (Luke 2:52) and admitted ignorance on certain matters (Matt. 24:36). These limitations do not eliminate the possibility of moral perfection; they simply indicate the human need for constant reliance on God and the indwelling of the Holy Spirit. In other words, they indicate the need for participation in the divine nature.

To strive for moral perfection, then, does not necessitate overcoming legitimate human limitations. Humans can be everything that God intended for and designed us to be even with such limitations. Moral perfection is not a matter of transcending natural human limitations but a matter of being taken up in a relationship with God—to participate in the divine nature.

5

Holiness and the Nature and Problem of Sin

Like so many other kids, my best friends and I spent many Saturday afternoons at the local theater, taking in low-budget matinees. Having spent the lion's share of our entire week's allowance on admission, a soft drink, and a huge bag of popcorn, we would find our way into the auditorium to enjoy whatever movie happened to be playing that week: old comedies, cartoon features, martial arts pictures, stale military epics. We didn't care what was playing, since we were just happy to be there. Our eyes riveted to the giant screen before us, we wanted to take it all in and not miss a thing. When the show was over and the lights came on, we would make our way through the exit doors and onto the streets of downtown. The trip home would be spent regaling one another by quoting iconic lines or reenacting particularly memorable scenes from whatever we had just seen. We kept one another in stitches the whole way home.

Everything changed in the summer of 1975. Our band of now preteen boys, feeling a little more mature than our actual age, decided to spend a little more money to see the new block-buster that everyone was talking about. Best known for its slow, pulsating, foreboding, and haunting John Williams soundtrack (*bah-da, bah-da, bah-da*) and its nonhuman, mechanical villain Bruce, the movie was, of course, *Jaws*.[1] This time, when the show was over and the lights came on, our troop still made its way through the exit doors and onto the streets of downtown, but there was little regaling going on. All we dared to say was (you guessed it) *bah-da, bah-da, bah-da* as one of us would lunge out quickly to grab someone else.

What set this movie apart from those we had previously seen—beyond the increased cost of admission, the increased age of the average patron, and the increased intensity of the subject matter—was the way it was promoted. Typically when a name appeared on the marquee for a movie, it was the name of the hero or protagonist, the one that you were cheering for. This movie was different. The name on the marquee was simply *Jaws*. While the shark was neither the hero nor the antihero, it was the villain whose actions precipitated the entire plot. And although there is no kind of redemption for it, the shark was in many ways the focal point of the movie.

Similarly in discussions of holiness, we can often make the focal point not God or Christ but that which is heinous, vile, unholy, ugly, and unredeemable: sin. We put *sin* on the marquee in order to attract attention. Yet, as argued in the preceding chapters, holiness is not so much about avoiding sin as it is about participating in the divine. We thus have rightly made our focus God's nature and the ways in which God's image is reflected in humanity. Nevertheless, as we saw in the previous chapter, sin has tarnished the *imago dei* in humanity, and so it plays an unavoidable role in any discussion of holiness. While being careful to avoid making sin the focal point, we would do well to understand it properly. If we do not start with an accurate understanding of the depth, breadth, and complexity of sin, we will be hindered in our struggle against it, and our pursuit of holiness will be unsuccessful. In this chapter, then, we seek a biblically grounded and theologically sound understanding of sin, not for its own sake but in order to understand its relationship to our true focal point: holiness.

Biblical Language for Sin

In chapter 3 we discussed holiness in relation to God and God's attributes. It is important to keep this understanding of holiness at the forefront of our minds as we discuss the nature of sin, since sin is ultimately nothing more than that which exists in opposition to God. Sin is not a positive entity but is fundamentally parasitic; it gains its identity and definition through its relation to God, even if this relation is a strictly antagonistic one. Whether it is understood to be contrary to God's nature or will, sin's identity is grounded in its distinction from him. And just as we saw that human language is inadequate to fully describe God's nature (chap. 3 excursus), so too we must acknowledge that the nature of sin is mysterious and beyond the capacity of human words to describe fully. Thus, in order to paint as full a picture as possible of the many ways in which sin is contrary to God, Scripture employs a large number of terms, concepts, metaphors, and images to refer to sin. Here I will focus on five major ways in which Scripture describes sin: missing the mark, irreligion, transgression, rebellion, and perversion.[2]

Missing the Mark

The most common way to refer to sin in Scripture is through the idea of *missing the mark*, not pursuing what one should. In the Old Testament, this idea is communicated by the Hebrew verb *ḥāṭā'*, which is used over six hundred times.[3] In the New Testament, the same idea is communicated by the use of the Greek word *hamartanō*. Like its Old Testament counterpart, this concept is the most popular of all of the New Testament metaphors for sin.[4] The idea of missing the mark does not refer to a lack of talent or a failure to hit a target. The reason missing the mark is condemnable is that, rather than directing our effort and skill toward the target that God has prescribed, we have chosen to aim in a direction of our own choosing. To miss the mark is not the result of poor aim or poor execution; it is choosing to set for oneself the standard and goal after which one will strive. Missing the mark, whether expressed in the Hebrew *ḥāṭā'* or the Greek *hamartanō*, is not a matter of human weakness but is a willful act of self-determination for which humans are culpable.[5]

Irreligion

The charge of *irreligion*, not worshiping what one should, stood as a stark and outlandish accusation in a world that was permeated by religion. As noted in chapter 2, the Roman world was a veritable supermarket of religious ideas with temples and shrines at every turn. Irreligion was unheard of. The question was not whether one was religious but to which religion or religions a person subscribed. When Scripture makes the charge of irreligion, it doesn't mean that the accused didn't worship anything. Instead, the charge of irreligion was directed at those who rejected the true religion revealed in the character of the world that God has made, the story of Israel, the Scriptures, and, most vividly, the person of Jesus Christ.

In the New Testament, a variety of negative terms (as indicated by the prefix *a-*) are used to communicate the idea of *ir*religion—each with its own nuance. *Asebeia* denotes a lack of worship, a godlessness, an irreverence, and an impiety[6] (e.g., Rom. 1:18; Titus 2:12; Jude 15, 18). *Adikia* refers to an absence of righteousness and, in particular, the neglect of one's duty before God (e.g., Luke 13:27; Rom. 6:13; 1 John 1:9).[7] *Anomia*, simply translated "lawlessness," refers to the sinful behavior of both those who are ignorant of the law of God and those who live as though there were no such law (e.g., Rom. 6:19; Titus 2:14; 1 John 3:4).[8] The charge of *anomia* was not so much about breaking any single law in particular as it was about disregarding the righteousness and goodness of the law of God and of God himself.

Transgression

The idea of *transgression* is conveyed in the Old Testament by the word *'ābar*, which, like *ḥāṭā'*, is also found over six hundred times. In most cases this word is used in the literal sense of "crossing over" or "passing by."[9] When used in this way, it does not carry any ethical connotations. Yet it is also used to refer to "overstepping one's rightful limits," "disregarding proper limitations," or "violating a law," especially as these are understood in relation to the commands of the Lord (e.g., Deut. 17:2; Jer. 34:18; Hosea 6:7). Such people dare to go where they should not. The same notion is found in the New Testament, where the Greek term *parabainō* is used to describe "the violation of a [divine] directive" (e.g., Rom. 2:23; 5:14; Gal. 3:19; Heb. 2:2).[10] Scripture's use of "transgression" could be understood to mean trampling the law of God underfoot or crossing a line that God has drawn in the sand.[11] The idea applies to transgressing both particular laws and the law of God in general.[12]

Related to the idea of transgression is the idea of iniquity (*'āwôn* in Hebrew), "the idea of twisting or distortion."[13] Iniquity refers to deviation from a true and right course or failure to fulfill the requirements of justice and to hold a straight and impartial approach. In particular, it means humanity's failure to fulfill the law of God. This charge is particularly used against the people of God when the attitudes they hold and the actions they take do not align with their identity as God's people.

Rebellion

Another common biblical idea is *rebellion*, serving someone other than the person or God who should be served. It is especially common in the Old Testament, where it is used in reference to fathers, kings, and God. This concept is represented by various Hebrew terms: *pešaʿ* (Job 13:23; Ps. 103:12), *mārâ* (Num. 20:24; Ezek. 20:13), and *mārad* (Dan. 9:5; Josh. 22:16). While there are differences of nuance among these terms, each indicates the idea of turning against a right and fitting allegiance. Fueling this turning is stubborn self-interest, self-determination, and self-aggrandizement. In the New Testament, the word *apeitheia* likewise refers to disobedience to those in authority. Most often it is used of humanity's relationship with God (e.g., Eph. 2:2; Heb. 4:6).[14] While it is sometimes used to refer to believers, one of its main uses in the New Testament is to refer to the failure of unbelievers to respond positively to the gospel. Paul writes, for example, that the gentiles, who have the law written in creation and on their hearts, have rejected God and are therefore rebellious (Rom. 1:19–20; 2:14–15).

Where rebellion is a breach of duty and proper allegiance, treason (Hebrew *ma'al* and *bāgad*) is a breach of trust, a deliberate turning from the good to which one has been exposed and that one has espoused (Lev. 26:40; Ezek. 14:13; 15:8). The Greek word for treason, *parapiptō* (literally, "to fall away"), refers to "a deliberate turning from what one has been exposed to and has partaken of" (e.g., Heb. 6:6).[15] In relation to God, sin is treasonous in the sense that those who have experienced the manifold blessings that flow from relationship with him have knowingly rejected him for another. What makes this kind of treason especially vile and culpable is that it is committed against the one who is all-loving and good.

Perversion

The concept of *perversion* connotes being bent or twisted. It is to see and do things in ways other than how one should. The Hebrew word that communicates this idea in the Old Testament is *'āwôn* (Lev. 16:21–22; Ps. 51:2),[16] and in the New Testament it is conveyed with the Greek word *diastrephō* (Matt. 17:17; Acts 13:10).[17] Humans show their perversion whenever they behave in a way that is contrary to their being created in God's image. This is especially so when humans distort judgment of justice and of right and wrong (Isa. 19:14; 21:3) and when they malign the gospel (Acts 13:10).[18] Perversion encompasses every aspect of sin's nature: its cause, its character, and its result.

A particularly vile kind of perversion is an *abomination*. In Hebrew this idea is represented by three words—*piggûl*, *šiqqûṣ*, and *tô'ēbâ*[19]—each conveying a varying degree of repulsion, with the last being the most repugnant and serious (Gen. 46:34;

Deut. 7:25, 26). In the New Testament, the Greek term *bdelygma* is used to denote an "abomination" or "detestable thing" (e.g., Matt. 24:15; Luke 16:15; Rev. 17:4, 5).[20] Throughout Scripture, an abomination is anything that is especially reprehensible, repugnant, and offensive, especially to God. Sin in general is an abomination to God, though some sins are singled out as being especially so, eliciting from him an especially fierce response. As Millard Erickson writes, "These practices virtually nauseate God."[21]

A Mosaic Understanding of Sin

In fine arts, a mosaic is an image or a pattern that is formed by an artist's selection and arrangement of diverse pieces of tile, glass, or other material. Within a mosaic, the texture, color, and shape of each aspect play significant roles in defining the larger image. No single piece, no matter how large, is sufficient in itself to convey the full picture; yet each piece, no matter how small, contributes to the shape and definition of the whole. Ultimately, it is only through the distinct contributions of all the pieces that the larger picture takes its full, rich, and final shape. While they often express very distinct images, mosaics by their very nature do not have the same clarity and definition that other forms of art, such as photography, exhibit.

The task of defining the nature of sin is a complex one. No single metaphor, even a biblical one, is rich enough to encompass the breadth and depth of Scripture's testimony regarding it. Sin defies a simple definition. Given its shadowy and negative existence in relation to the person, role, and will of God, sin is beyond the ability of simple identification and explanation. The mystery of sin is not merely that of a puzzle we have yet to solve; it is a mystery beyond the capacity of human language to fully express.

To overcome the innate inadequacy of human language and to define the mystery that we have labeled "sin," I suggest that we take advice from art. Rather than trying to provide a precise definition of sin, we can attempt to create a mosaic of what sin is like from each of the metaphors above. Like a mosaic, the fuller picture may not be as sharply defined as we may want it to be. But viewing these various aspects together provides us with a larger and fuller picture of sin than any one of the aspects can on its own, thereby keeping us from having too small a picture of sin.

Having discussed a number of biblical metaphors for sin that make up our mosaic understanding, we are now in a position to be able to step back and describe our picture as a whole. While each of the metaphors makes its own unique contribution to the mosaic, the metaphors together communicate some bigger themes. Here we will discuss three main themes: sin as willful, as relational, and as an attack on God.

Sin Is Willful

While it may be most explicit in the term *hamartia*, the idea that sin is willful is found in each of the scriptural metaphors. We sometimes like to think of sin as an accident or the unfortunate result of a series of random events, but Scripture teaches that we enter into sin in an intentional and willful act. Not only was this the case in the garden of Eden; it remains the case even after the fall. Whether one stands with Martin Luther's *The Bondage of the Will* or Desiderius Erasmus's *The Freedom of the Will*, the will is engaged in the conception, birth, and act of sin. While our wills may be ill-informed and even depraved, and while our consciences may have become calloused and grown insensitive by our habitual sin (Rom. 1:21), it remains true that sin is always both considered and chosen. Sin is not merely something we do; it is something that we think about and plan for. Though our reasoning may be faulty, we enter into sin willfully and often provide justification for it. The willful character of sin only adds to its diabolicalness, treachery, and abominableness.

Sin Is Relational

Humanity is an essentially relational creature. As we saw in chapter 4, humans were created to be the image of a God who is essentially and eternally relational. The lone aspect of creation that God pronounced "not good" was that man was alone (Gen. 2:18). Given that humanity is so fundamentally relational, we should not be surprised to find that sin has maligned humanity's ability to relate rightly. Sin is an attack on and a diminishment of proper human relationships.[22]

Sin disfigures every relationship for which humanity was created.[23] With the introduction of sin in Genesis 3, the breakdown of relationships follows immediately. We witness sin's effect on the divine–human relationship in Adam and Eve's attempt to hide from God and in their eviction from the garden. We see the consequence of sin on the human–human relationship in Adam's blaming of Eve and in the changed relationship that would exist between the man and the woman. Finally, we see the consequences of sin on the creation–human relationship through the rise of thorns and thistles and the significant toil that it would take for humans to survive off the land.

The effects of sin on the divine–human relationship are profound. While sin has dire consequences for all areas of human relationships, it has been particularly destructive here. Sin not only attempts to destroy this relationship; it also challenges the propriety of the relationship. Sin seeks to seize those rights and roles that are rightfully the creator's alone. Sin challenges the righteousness of the decisions and forms established by God. Sin is an abuse of the prerogatives given to those who are created in the *imago dei*. Following the incursion of sin in the world, humanity is now at enmity with God (Rom. 8:7).

Sin injures human–human relationships in two distinct ways. First, sin breaks down the relationships among humans. The immediate preparation of the fig-leaf coverings following sin in the garden (Gen. 3:7) speaks of the mutual suspicion of the sexes. This breakdown is also revealed in Adam's response when God confronts them with their sin. In seven short words, Adam blames every other moral being in all existence for his sin: "The *woman you* put here with me . . ." (Gen. 3:12; emphasis added). Not only does he blame Eve for his sin, thus distancing himself from her; he also indirectly blames God for putting her there with him. In his curse on the woman, God states that sin will result in a disharmony between the man and the woman, where before there was only cooperation (Gen. 3:16).

Second, sin causes humans to suffer a breakdown within the self, a dissolution of proper internal workings. Sin both fosters and is the consequence of humans' inherent ability to self-deceive. As my father once told me, the easiest person to fool in any room is oneself. Jeremiah's denial of humanity's ability to plumb the depths of the human heart is directed not only at the enigma that is the human race in general but also at the heart of each individual (Jer. 17:9). Jesus's accusation concerning those who could detect the smallest speck in the eyes of others but could not see the log in their own eyes shows the reality and the absurdity of self-deceit (Matt. 7:3). Strangely, humanity seems especially liable to self-deceit in those moments where it is considering its own righteousness and holiness (James 1:22, 26).

In addition to affecting divine–human and human–human relationships, sin affects the creation–human relationship. After Adam and Eve's sin in the garden, the creation into which humanity was placed—a creation that originally was particularly fitted for its occupancy—became a far less hospitable, and at times even an adversarial, place to live (Gen. 3:17b–19).

Sin skews humans' perception of creation and of humanity's relation to it, often in one of two ways. At one end of the spectrum, rather than lovingly caring for it in the same way God does, humans have treated creation as nothing more than a commodity to be used solely for its personal gratification or pleasure. More and more, Christians are condemning such an attitude as a corruption of what it means for humanity to have dominion over creation (Gen. 1:26). It fails to replicate God's love for creation and his desire for its flourishing, thus perverting the idea of dominion and corrupting what it means to be created in God's image.[24] At the other end of the spectrum, rather than worshiping God alone, humans have elevated creation to an object of worship. Such idolatry is uniformly and strongly condemned throughout the Scriptures, perhaps no more clearly than in the opening chapter of Paul's Epistle to the Romans, where Paul writes that humans have "worshiped and served created things rather than the Creator" (Rom. 1:25).

Sin Is an Attack on God

In addition to its willful and relational character, sin is fundamentally an attack on God. God is creator of and sovereign over the entire universe, and any sin committed under his rule and within his realm—no matter whom the intended object may appear to be—is thus an offense against God.[25] Two biblical accounts, one from the Old Testament and one from the New, illustrate this idea especially well. After being confronted for abusing his status as king to sleep with Bathsheba and then to order her husband, Uriah, to be killed in battle, King David makes what might appear to be a strange confession: "I have sinned *against the Lord*" (2 Sam. 12:13; emphasis added). This confession is made in even starker terms in his famous prayer: "Against you, *you only*, have I sinned" (Ps. 51:4; emphasis added). David's sin was obviously directed at other humans, but he understood it as fundamentally an attack on God.

The book of Acts provides another striking example. At the end of Acts 4, we are told that the new believers were sharing everything they had with one another. Some were even selling property and sharing the proceeds with one another, and as a result "there were no needy persons among them" (Acts 4:34). One couple, Ananias and Sapphira, also sold a piece of property and brought much of the proceeds from the sale to the apostles to be distributed among the community. However, we are told that Ananias, with his wife's full knowledge, "kept back part of the money for himself" (Acts 5:2). Rather than taking Ananias's greed as a sin against the community, Peter tells Ananias, "You have not lied just to human beings but to God" (Acts 5:4). When Sapphira likewise lies about the money, Peter asks her how she can "conspire to test the Spirit of the Lord" (Acts 5:9). Once again, an act that had ramifications on human relations is seen as fundamentally an affront to God.

Often our language reveals that we consider the object of our sin to be the law rather than God. While sin is rightly understood as a breach of the law and thus might be said to be "against the law," the law is not something that can be sinned against per se. The law has no existence apart from God. In Christian theology, the law is understood as a reflection of the person and character of God and thus as his expectations for his creation and particularly for humanity.[26] The law of God, especially in the Old Testament, gained its importance not from its own righteous character but from its being the "law *of the* LORD" (Lev. 26:43; 2 Kings 10:31; emphasis added).

Scripture is clear that God is the object of sin, but it is just as clear that God is not always the sole object of sin. On numerous occasions, Scripture indicates that sin had as its intended object someone other than God (e.g., 1 Sam. 2:25; Isa. 64:5; Matt. 6:14; 18:21; Luke 11:4; 15:21; 17:3; 1 Cor. 8:12). How can we reconcile these two clear but seemingly contradictory pictures? What, for example, are we to make of David's statement? Is it hyperbole, the understandable exaggeration of a man who has just been confronted by a prophet of God regarding his blatant and vile sin? Is it an expression of David's understanding of God's prerogatives and privileges as the eternal sovereign? Perhaps. There may be, however, another way to understand it. As has been noted numerous times previously, humans are created in God's image. Since humanity was created this way, any sin directed against another human is ultimately a sin against the one whose image that human bears. By the design and grace of God, humanity stands as God's representative in creation. Therefore, just as an attack on an agent of the state is understood as an attack on the very state that the agent represents, so too an attack on the image of God may be rightly understood as an affront to the God whom that image signifies.[27] In Genesis 9:6, for example, the treachery of murder is tied not to its social consequences or to the loss of the life that was taken. Murder,

God declares, gains its seriousness from the fact that humanity, even fallen humanity, is made in the *imago dei*.

EXCURSUS: **Political Correctness, Tolerance, and Holiness**

We live in a world where political correctness and tolerance are among the most highly regarded of social virtues. Political correctness—defined as "relating to, or supporting broad social, political, and educational change, especially to redress historical injustices in matters such as race, class, gender, and sexual orientation"[28]—often manifests itself in the avoidance of language or actions that could be considered to denigrate, disregard, or exclude anyone who may be perceived to have been disadvantaged and discriminated against. Likewise, tolerance is an "interest in and concern for ideas, opinions, practices, etc., [that are] foreign to one's own; a liberal, undogmatic viewpoint."[29] It is, in short, to live and let live.

Recent world history is the story of the gross violence of bigotry and blind dogmatism. The twentieth and twenty-first centuries are replete with accounts of violent racism, unfathomable genocides, and brutal fascisms. In sober retrospect, contemporary society has rejected such positions and promoted more temperate views on a wide variety of subjects. Regrettably, Christians are not immune from supporting, participating in, and even leading some of these atrocious movements, many of which tragically employ Scripture and a monstrous form of Christian theology to support and promote detestable ideologies. As a result, contemporary Christians need to be modest and discerning in regard to the positions they hold dogmatically because even the best of people and the best of causes are not beyond the realm of corruption, even when they bear the name of Christ. This includes the belief that the practices

of other people and cultures are sinful or even downright diabolical simply in virtue of their otherness. Yet, just as not all
common Christian practices are necessarily sanctified, so too
not all forms of otherness are necessarily sinful.

Most religions, philosophies, and cultures affirm the existence of sin. While each calls it something distinct and defines
and nuances it differently, most affirm some form of evil exists
and that humans often engage in behavior contrary to that
which should be the norm. In spite of very real differences,
this common ground provides the church with a platform from
which to engage those around it on this profound religious and
theological concept. To assert that sin exists, therefore, may not
be as politically incorrect, intolerant, or exclusively Christian
as one might be tempted to think.

At the same time, there is a very real threat that the virtues of
political correctness and tolerance will lead the church to remain
silent on issues that ought to be brought forward and discussed,
lest Christians be branded politically incorrect or intolerant.
Regrettably, the desire to appear politically correct and tolerant can lead society to insist that *nothing* may be rightly and
assuredly identified as sin. All actions, opinions, and motives
become relative, and the existence of sin is practically denied.
In contrast, the Christian faith not only asserts that sin exists
but that sin has a particular source, nature, and manifestation.
Furthermore, for Christians sin finds its definition not primarily
in contrast to virtues, rules, regulations, or laws but in contrast to
the nature and character of God. For the Christian, sin is not so
much speculative and theoretical as it is personal and relational.

Living in a God-Shrinking World

According to J. I. Packer, "The life of true holiness is rooted
in the soil of awed adoration" of the grandeur of God and his

works of salvation.[30] The particular picture of God that Packer has in mind is today branded as intolerant, narrow-minded, and inconsistent with the norms of contemporary culture. The proposed solution is to deny either that there is a singular definition of God or that there is any God at all. In practice, such a position leaves God out of the picture. If such an attitude allows for the possibility of a God, its tendency is to tame God into a character who may be liked but who is neither to be feared nor to be held in awe. He is a small god and, therefore, a god who may be followed or not as one should choose. A god that cannot inspire awe, however, is a god who cannot inspire holiness.

Living in a Sin-Shrinking World

The world in which we live is a world where the idea of sin too is diminishing. As eminent American psychiatrist Karl Menninger observes, "The very word 'sin,' which seems to have disappeared, was a proud word. It was once a strong word, an ominous and serious word. It described a central point in every civilized human being's life plan and life style. But the word went away. It has almost disappeared—the word, along with the notion."[31] What used to be identified as sin and, therefore, viewed as a matter of significant consequence, is today rarely identified as much more than an alternative ethic, an embarrassment, or a mistake.

Given the lack of gravity accorded to sin, coupled with the lack of awe accorded to God, is it any wonder that sin no longer produces shame, regret, fear, or pain for many? Sin is no longer understood to be an act of ultimate treason or treachery against the holy, pure, and loving creator and sovereign of the universe. In contrast, Christian theology has treated sin with utmost seriousness precisely because of its antithetical relation to the character of the magnificent God against whom it is an affront. When this perspective is lost, sin can no longer carry any significant, let alone eternal, consequences.

In a world with a diminished view of both God and sin, discussions of holiness are believed to be irrelevant and uninteresting. Regrettably, such "God-shrinking" and "sin-shrinking" happens not only in the world but also in the church, where the idea of God is often shrunk from the portrait painted by Scripture to the point that Jesus, the eternal Son, the one in whom all things have their being and hold together, may now be understood as little more than my "homeboy" (as one popular T-shirt describes him). As a result, sin too has lost its gravity in the church, where it is now tolerated even within the fellowship. Such an attitude is evident in the church's reluctance to engage in church discipline, to actively promote holiness, and to hold its people to a higher standard of behavior than that found on the street.

6

Holiness and the Nature and Goal of Salvation

Every culture has its own idioms and accent, even if it shares the same language with other cultures. As a western Canadian who did graduate studies in New Jersey, for example, I learned quickly that my neighbors and I were not always speaking the same language, even though we all apparently spoke English! This holds true within the academy as well, where each academic discipline has its own jargon. Theology is no different. The mastery and the memorization of the jargon—the technical terms employed by particular disciplines, trades, or professions—cause many students great anxiety. Consequently, many protest the seeming needlessness of big words to communicate ideas that much smaller words could capably handle. In feigned sympathy I often respond, "Yes, why does theology feel the need to use big words like *supralapsarianism*, *modalistic monarchianism*, and *Amyraldianism*, when the very same ideas could be communicated by simpler words? Why can't theology be more like botany? After all, botany is satisfied to talk about that process whereby plants convert sunlight, carbon dioxide, and water into food energy through the use of chlorophyll without the use of big words. Botany doesn't feel the need to develop jargon for that!" The trap has been set. Inevitably a student will shout, "That's called photosynthesis!" In contrived incredulity, I respond, "No! Photosynthesis? That has five syllables! No one can possibly be expected to remember such a big word. You must not have picked up on that until college." Without realizing he is entering further into the trap, the respondent will often note that he actually learned that back in middle school. By this time most of my students get the point: mastering jargon not only is possible but also serves the helpful purpose of verbal efficiency—one larger word can communicate what would otherwise take a long list of shorter and often less precise words.

Since this book is intended to be an introduction to the theology of holiness, I have avoided the unnecessary use of jargon. But if there were ever a time to utilize jargon, it would be in this chapter on the relation of holiness and salvation. For it seems to me that the disinterest in holiness within the evangelical church is not so much the result of a creeping secularism or liberalism as it is a truncated and faulty theology of salvation. If I were to give in to the temptation to use theological jargon, I might assert that the basic problem with so much of popular evangelical theology is that it has a *soteriology* with an *eschatology* but with very little *teleology*. That is, popular evangelical theology has an understanding of salvation (*soteriology*) that thinks about—and, at times, obsesses over—the order of the culminating events of history (*eschatology*) but rarely considers the question of what God's goal (*teleology*) for humanity might be. For far too long, evangelical teaching on salvation has been excessively focused on the question of "spiritual geography"—the question of where humans (saved and unsaved) will spend eternity—and has practically abandoned what I would suggest are more fundamental questions: What is God's purpose and goal for humanity itself? What is humanity to become? This is especially puzzling since the primary testimony of Scripture is not about eschatology but about *ontology*—the kind of being that humans are to be. In the end, Scripture is less concerned with *where* humans will end up than with *what* humans will become.

Being concerned with where one will spend eternity is, of course, completely understandable. The vivid depictions that Scripture gives of the afterlife should lead anyone to carefully consider such things. The question of eternal destiny is integral to the gospel and to the whole counsel of God and is thus worthy of consideration. I don't intend to downplay the question of spiritual geography. Rather, I suggest that the common evangelical understanding of this as the most important—if not the only—question in regard to human destiny is biblically unwarranted and pastorally unhelpful. The goal of salvation is not merely to make it to heaven but "to be like God in true righteousness and holiness" (Eph. 4:24). In short, there is a necessary and integral relationship between salvation and holiness, as can be seen in a number of biblical concepts used to describe salvation.

Biblical Language for Salvation

Just as Scripture employs numerous terms to describe sin, so too it uses several concepts to describe salvation, God's gracious response to sin. The depth and nature of God's response to sin is as unique and mysterious as is sin itself. The concepts and metaphors used to describe salvation come from a range of areas of human experience: legal, biological, commercial, religious, and so on. Yet while each of these concepts describes a different aspect of God's saving work, and while each comes from a different realm of human experience, each relates salvation directly to holiness. In every case, the concept is linked either to holiness's transcendent aspect or to its moral aspect, while in some cases it speaks to both. Here we will briefly look at four major ways that Scripture describes salvation before taking a closer look at a fifth concept that has its own peculiarities.

Foreknowledge

One way that Scripture speaks of God's gracious work for a sinful humanity is *foreknowledge*. Foreknowledge speaks of the power and intent of God in relation to creation so that what he knows actually comes to pass and what comes to pass is what he has known. In relation to salvation, God foreknows those to whom he will apply his gracious response to sin. He foreknows those he will save and who will be in relationship with him. Theologically speaking, foreknowledge is more than just God's awareness of those events that will come to pass and the identity of those who will be saved. It means more than that he has determined to bring such things about. It means he intends that such things will happen and, given his sovereignty, almightiness, and wisdom, that such things will indeed occur.[1] It also means that God intends and will bring about holiness, in both its aspects, within those made in his image. God's foreknowledge intends and will secure a change in both human behavior and human status. Those who are saved will be "blameless" (Eph. 1:4), "obedient" (1 Pet. 1:2), and "conformed to the image of his

Son" (Rom. 8:29), as well as possess "sonship" (Eph. 1:5) and
be "sanctified" (1 Pet. 1:2).

Election

The second concept, *election*, expresses the idea that God not
only knows who will be the recipients of his gracious response
to the debilitating effects of sin but also has chosen them for
that very purpose. Election implies that not all are chosen. This
distinguishes the elect—those who have been so chosen—from
all others. The biblical concept of election indicates that God's
choice of these people issues substantially and entirely from
within himself; it is unconditional, based on his own unfathomable will. It is therefore not based on the merit, suitability, or
attractiveness of those who are elected. While we cannot know
why he has elected whom he has, we can know that it was not
based on any characteristic of those elected.

Moreover, election has a goal, or *telos*, beyond itself. God
does not just select or gather some people to himself; he elects
them with a purpose: holiness. They are given a distinct status
as God's "special possession" (1 Pet. 2:9), "appointed" (John
15:16), and "first fruits" (2 Thess. 2:13), but they also elect to
live in a particular way—to "declare his praises" (1 Pet. 2:9), to
be "holy and dearly loved" (Col. 3:12–17), to "go and bear fruit"
(John 15:16), which includes compassion, kindness, humility,
gentleness, patience, forgiveness, peaceableness, thankfulness,
and "belief in the truth" (Col. 3:12–17; 2 Thess. 2:13).

Regeneration

Third, the biological metaphor *regeneration*, which means
"to be born again" or "to be made anew," speaks to the idea

113

of life. This is the metaphor that Jesus uses to talk about salvation when meeting at night with Nicodemus (John 3:1–21). It denotes how God deals with humans who are spiritually dead and therefore helpless.[2] Regeneration describes the drastic new beginning and new life that God provides for those who were previously spiritually dead. It is not merely the extension of the previous human "life" but is the beginning of a new, higher kind of life. As with the previous concepts, regeneration has to do with holiness, in the sense of both status or nature and the actions appropriate to one so born. So, for example, Peter calls those who have been saved "children," implying their unique status, and then goes on to list how children are to act: "obedient," "not conform[ing] to evil desires," showing "sincere love for one another," and so on (1 Pet. 1:13–23).[3]

Redemption

Redemption is a metaphor that moves our attention to the market. Redemption implies that God has paid a price to obtain those who are his. This is true even when there is no explicit tie between the act of redemption and the identification of the payment that was made.[4] This metaphor implies that those who are now with God were once enslaved to an illegitimate master and that God has provided for their release. It does not mean that those once enslaved are now on their own. Instead, they are now slaves to God, as they were bought by him, and therefore they are slaves to righteousness (Rom. 6:18–22). Scripture ties closely together the concept of redemption to the idea of holiness. The redeemed belong to God and, consequently, are to act in a way that befits that relationship. Because of their redemption, they have a status that is distinct from the rest of humanity, and therefore they are to conduct themselves differently. This metaphor, as with the other biblical concepts discussed above, identifies the goal of God's saving work as holiness, in both its transcendent and its ethical meanings.

The Strange Case of Justification

Another of Scripture's metaphors for God's saving work in humanity is *justification*. While this metaphor appears throughout the New Testament, it plays a particularly significant role in Paul's writings,[5] especially his Epistle to the Romans. Justification is a legal or forensic metaphor and describes the work of God whereby he qualifies people to stand before him, the righteous judge,[6] free from the guilt and penalty of sin.

While this metaphor is found in the New Testament and utilized throughout the Christian tradition, its prominence in current discussions of salvation among Protestants is due in no small part to German Reformer Martin Luther (1483–1546). It is said that Luther, tormented by an overwhelming sense of personal guilt before God's law and a foreboding sense of his own doom, was driven to search the Scriptures, seeking to discover the basis on which God justified sinners such as himself. Following his close study of Romans and especially his "discovery" of Romans 1:17,[7] Luther concluded that rather than meriting justification through personal acts of piety, as he had always believed, he was justified by the grace of God alone (*sola gratia*), a grace that was received through faith alone (*sola fide*). This justification was based in no way on one's merit (present, past, or future) but on the merit of Christ alone (*solus Christus*). On Luther's understanding, justification is the gracious declaration of God whereby, on the basis of the merit of Christ alone, sinful humans are pardoned in regard to the law.

For Luther, those to whom this work of God is applied exist in a state of paradox. In the present age, such people are *simul justus et peccator*—simultaneously justified and sinners.[8] Luther was not suggesting merely that these people have their good moments (justified) and their bad moments (sinners). Instead, he meant that those who are objects of God's grace are at one and the same time both justified (by the gracious declaration of God, based on the merits of Christ, received by faith) and sinners (by their own nature and behavior).

So central was this understanding of justification to Luther's own theology (and to his personal spiritual relief) that for him and his theological progeny the doctrine of justification became the linchpin of the gospel itself. It was, as he called it, "the principal doctrine of Christianity."[9] To compromise on this point, he said, would be to jeopardize everything.[10] He argued that if this doctrine stands, the church stands; if it falls, the church falls.[11] Even more, he believed that this particular doctrine of justification was "the touchstone by which we can judge most surely and freely about all doctrines, works, forms of worship, and ceremonies of all men."[12] For Luther, this understanding of justification became the filter through which all Scripture must be strained or the rule by which all Scripture must be interpreted.

Protestantism in general and evangelicalism in particular have remained steadfastly loyal to Luther in this area. What this means is that justification reigns in these traditions as the undisputed and absolute king of the salvation metaphors. It is viewed not merely as one component of God's saving work among others or merely as one way to understand how God saves. Rather, justification is viewed as though it were synonymous with salvation. To be justified *is* to be saved (and vice versa). Consequently, many evangelicals view salvation solely in forensic terms. The entirety of God's saving work is found in addressing one's legal standing. Since justification is understood to be independent of human nature and behavior, it is concluded that salvation has no necessary relation to holiness. Such a view leaves humanity not only with nothing to contribute to its salvation but effectively with no obligation in response to it either.[13]

At least three problems accompany this approach to the understanding of justification. The first is a historical one: some have argued that the popular picture of Luther's theology, as described above, is little more than a caricature. Without denying the pivotal role that justification played in Luther's theology, they assert that Luther's understanding was not as narrow and exclusive as we have been led to believe. Instead, they note that Luther's understanding of justification, while undeniably including the concept of forensic declaration and emphasizing the graciousness of God and the inability of humanity, was not as completely and absolutely separated from the idea of holiness as it has so often been understood to be.[14]

The second problem is that it suffers the consequences of what has been called "metaphoric myopia"[15]—the privileging of one metaphor above all others. Questions of Luther historiography aside, this problem lies in how those who adhere to justification as the primary metaphor of salvation often either ignore the other biblical metaphors or force them to conform to justification's mold, requiring them to say what it says and nothing more. Each metaphor is thereby stripped of its distinct meaning and contribution.[16] The understanding of salvation that results is a diminished understanding that cannot convey the fullness of biblical teaching. Even if a single metaphor is central to the gospel and has a special ability to shed light on divine mystery, it cannot be so esteemed that it diminishes the contributions of Scripture's other metaphors. In this case, a particular understanding of justification cannot be allowed to mute the distinctive voices of Scripture's other salvation metaphors. In spite of justification's proper emphasis on the gracious nature of God's saving work, it cannot be allowed to undercut those metaphors that identify a clear (though not causative) connection between salvation and holiness.

The third problem has to do with the popular understanding of Luther's definition of justification itself, namely, the idea that "justification" refers exclusively to the idea of declaration. While the judge's declaration in any trial is pivotal and definitive, Scripture's portrayal of God's gracious work of justification involves more than just his unilateral and objective alteration of the sinner's legal standing. As with the other concepts of salvation discussed above, the language that Scripture employs in relation to justification includes the idea of the renewal of the sinner's nature and behavior. The historic understanding of justification as God declaring the sinner righteous is fittingly justified, but justification involves more than a declaration. God's justifying work not only involves the objective legal reclassification of the sinner but also looks toward the alteration of the human's nature and ultimately the human's behavior too.

In the Old Testament, the word that is most often translated into English as "righteous" or "just" is *ṣedek*. In its most literal sense, it means to be "straight, rigid, [or] stiff,"[17] and it was associated with a righteousness based on actual uprightness and truth. It often included the concept of vindication—to clear one of accusation, blame, suspicion, or doubt not arbitrarily but with the support of proof. The ancient Near Eastern and Hebrew understanding of justification was not modeled on modern jurisprudence, its understanding of the law, or the contemporary role of the court. The search for justice in these ancient settings occurred at the gates of the city, the meeting place of the people, the site where the elders and other city officials would gather to hear cases of various kinds. The goal of these councils was not merely to seek a conviction or acquittal, a pronouncement of guilt or innocence. Instead, they sought to discern and only consequently to declare who was actually in the right—and therefore righteous.[18] In this way, to be justified was far more than just to have been so classified by authoritative declaration. To justify was to determine who was actually in the right. Justification was not solely about decision; it was about discernment. It was not solely about declaration; it was about vindication. Even in those cases where the Old Testament uses the word in the sense of a declaration of rightness or righteousness, it is not removed from a consideration of the actual facts of the case. In the ancient Near East, to be justified or declared righteous was never understood to be a fiction. It was always understood to be tied in some way to the actual state of affairs.

In the Septuagint, a third-century-BCE Greek translation of the Old Testament, *ṣedek* is rendered by the Greek word *dikaioō* in about 90 percent of its five hundred or so occurrences.[19] It should therefore come as no surprise that for the New Testament authors, for whom the Septuagint was Scripture, there was a strong link between their use of the term *dikaioō* and the Old Testament use of *ṣedek*. While *dikaioō* may be translated "to declare or pronounce to be righteous," for the New Testament authors *dikaioō* would carry with it the connotation "to show or exhibit to be in the right." Even in the New Testament, then, justification need not be absolutely divorced from considerations of human nature or human behavior.

It was only by disconnecting the biblical concept of justification from its ancient Near Eastern setting and transporting it into a Greco-Roman law court that the interpretation of justification as more strongly tied to a declaration and acquittal developed. While it is true that many theological concepts from the Old Testament are shaped and further nuanced in the New Testament (through what theologians often call "progressive revelation"), their earlier meanings are not thereby inverted or contradicted. In the case of justification, this means that the idea of declaration cannot be understood as completely divorced from the actual condition of human character and human behavior, as some interpreters following Luther have made it out to be. When God justifies, it is not a total fiction. As Peter Toon writes, "There is no escape from the fact that justification by faith means a changed life."[20] In the context of the present study, we might adapt Toon's statement slightly: there is no escape from the fact that salvation means holiness.

The Goal of Salvation: The Renewal and Thriving of the *Imago Dei*

I have argued that salvation is not merely a matter of declaring someone to be righteous, as in some popular understandings of justification, but is a matter of actually making someone so. In theology, the term that refers to the process whereby God makes something holy is *sanctification*. The term is used to refer to two distinct yet closely related things. First, there is the *positional* use of the term. When used in this way, sanctification refers to that gracious work of God whereby something's relation to him and status before him is altered. To be sanctified in this way means that God takes something for himself, setting

120

it apart for his purposes. In this sense, something is sanctified at the moment it comes into relation with him. While this is truly a kind of holiness, it is just the beginning and not the end of the process.

The term "sanctification" also has a *progressive* use. When the term is used in this way, it refers to God's work of making those things that are in relation with him suited for that new and special relation. When used in this way, sanctification refers to God's work of bringing the nature and character of that on which he has laid claim into alignment with its standing before him. Where the positional use of sanctification is sometimes called "objective," meaning that it does not necessarily result in an inner change in the person declared holy, the progressive use of sanctification is "subjective," which indicates that an actual change does take place in the person to which it is applied. As Paul writes, God works in believers to "present [them] holy in his sight, without blemish and free from accusation" (Col. 1:22).

Paul described the product of God's saving work in humanity in both the positional and progressive ways. There is a "new creation" (Gal. 6:15; 2 Cor. 5:17) that is "created . . . to do good works" (Eph. 2:10).[21] The model for this "new creation" and the standard of "good works" is not a collection of abstract principles, values, or ideals, no matter how lofty, but has a particular object, standard, goal, and prototype. The "new creation," the goal of God's saving work in humanity, is the *imago dei*.[22]

The goal of sanctification, and thus the goal of salvation more generally, is to overcome the disastrous effects of sin. While the effects of sin's encroachment into creation are myriad, among the most devastating are the effects on the pinnacle of the created order, the *imago dei*. While sin did not obliterate the *imago dei*,[23] it deeply disfigured it, rendering humanity unable to accurately reflect or imitate God as it was created to do.[24] Consequently, among God's gracious responses to the manifold and disastrous effects of sin, the restoration of humanity to God's original intent for it is central.[25] While Paul talks variably about the "new self" and the "new creation" that result from God's saving work, he notes that this self has a particular shape. Through the process of sanctification, humans are "created to be like God" (Eph. 4:24)[26] and "renewed in knowledge in the *image* of its Creator" (Col. 3:1; emphasis added). The "new self" and the "new creation" that result from God's saving work are nothing other than the restored *imago dei*.

As we saw in chapter 4, Scripture does not leave even the *imago dei* undefined. It provides a precise pattern, an optimal example, of the *imago dei* in the person of Jesus Christ. He is described as "in very nature God" (Phil. 2:6), "the image of the invisible God" (Col. 1:15), and even as "himself God" (John 1:18). God's gracious work of sanctification conforms its subjects to Jesus Christ himself, not to an abstract and faceless definition. Paul wrote that the goal of God's saving work is not merely that believers would be declared justified but that they would be "conformed to the image of his Son, that he might be the firstborn among many brothers and sisters" (Rom. 8:29).

Conformity to Christ is not limited to one aspect of the human constitution; it is wide-ranging. As divine holiness describes not simply an aspect of God but the whole of God, his nature and his actions, so too conformity to Christ has to do with the whole of human being, its nature and behavior. To be conformed to the Son means, first, to be conformed to his nature. As we saw in chapter 3, the church confesses that Jesus Christ is fully divine and fully human—together in what theologians call the "hypostatic union." While the hypostatic union is unique to Christ alone, the recipients of God's saving work are not only saved by Christ but *indwelt* by him. This means that, although renewed humans do not share the hypostatic union, they are brought into the divine through Christ so that it can truly be said that the divine indwells them and even animates them. Though never properly their own, as it is in the case of Jesus, the divine so deeply resides in them that Peter can boldly declare that they "participate in the divine nature" (2 Pet. 1:4). While they do not cease to be human, they live in a way far grander than they could on their own. By partaking of the divine nature, they move from the realm of the ordinary (*ḥōl*) to the realm of the extraordinary, the holy—the realm of *qdš*.

The believer's conformity to Christ and participation in the divine nature are not without profound and far-reaching consequences. Left to its own devices, the human mind is hostile to God and cannot submit to him (Rom. 8:7; see also John 14:17 and 1 Cor. 2:14). Conformity to Christ includes the renewing of the mind (Rom. 12:2) so that the believer can truly be said to have gained the "mind of Christ" (1 Cor. 2:16). To have the mind of Christ results in a disposition that is fundamentally different from that which existed previously. It is to have an attitude of humility before and obedience to God (Phil. 2:5–8). It is to have a mind that lives according to the Spirit and his leading (Rom. 8:4).

In being conformed to Christ, believers are also enabled to follow the one whom John calls "the way" (John 14:6). They are equipped to "know his voice" and to "follow him" (John 10:4). John notes that such behavior is not only possible but also required: "Whoever claims to live in him must live as Jesus did" (1 John 2:6). Conformity to Christ enables freedom from the "law of sin and death" (Rom. 8:2)[27] and from "the evil desires you had when you lived in ignorance" (1 Pet. 1:14). As noted earlier, it is not merely a freedom *from* but also a freedom *to*.[28] As Donald Alexander writes, those who are conformed to Christ, the image of the invisible God, are "now able to understand intelligibly and to obey responsibly God's commands."[29] To be conformed to Christ means that one is enabled to do good works (Eph. 2:10), to will and to do God's good purpose (Phil. 2:13; see also Rom. 8:28), and to be free to truly and fully be like Christ—free to truly and fully be the *imago dei*. Rightly understood, then, salvation has everything to do with holiness.

Toward a Fuller Understanding of Salvation

As we have seen in this chapter, Scripture's description of salvation is much richer and more profound than it is often understood to be. The basis of Christian salvation is far more than just a change in one's legal status. While justification plays an indispensable role in a Christian understanding of salvation, we have seen that salvation includes not only justification but also sanctification—making one holy. On this understanding, salvation is so much more than how it is typically described. First, it is more than the restoration of moral innocence. As we saw in chapter 4, the innocence of the garden cannot match the fullness of what God has done for humanity in Jesus Christ. Second, it is much more than just a restoration of relationship. While the advent of sin certainly alienated humanity from God, from creation, and from one another, and while the Christian notion of salvation certainly includes the restoration of these relationships (e.g., 2 Cor. 5:20), it is more than restored relationships. Third, salvation is far more than just a state of (eternal) bliss. The promise of Jesus and the testimony of Scripture is that Christian salvation will entail joy (e.g., Pss. 9:14; 13:5; 51:2; John 10:10; 1 Pet. 1:8–9). Yet Jesus is just as sure to note that the Christian life will also include trials and temptations on this side of the eschaton (e.g., Rom. 5:1–5; James 1:2; 1 Pet. 1:6; 4:12). Fourth, salvation is much more than just a get-out-of-jail-free card. While salvation certainly removes those who believe in Christ from the wrath of God, it is not merely the turning away of God's wrath (e.g., 1 John 2:2). While salvation may include each of these understandings to some degree, we have seen in this chapter that it is more than just the combination of all of these understandings. It is the process by which God makes humans holy.

EXCURSUS: **Legalism, License, and Liberty**

Modern evangelicalism has given rise to two popular, distinct, and competing understandings of the relation of holiness to salvation: legalism and license. Each view, at various times and in various places, has gained a significant and dedicated following. Yet when closely scrutinized, each view reveals that it significantly misunderstands the true nature and practice of holiness and, therefore, the proper relation of the two. Ultimately and ironically, even with best intentions, each disposition actually discourages the pursuit of holiness.

Legalism

With the term *legalism* I am referring to the fervent adherence to certain moral statutes for the sake of adherence alone. This attitude, while not exclusive to the contemporary age, has been particularly popular within evangelicalism for the past century.

125

In spite of its popularity, however, legalism misses the true nature of Christian salvation at its very core. Legalism confuses and inverts the proper relationship of two key aspects of Christian holiness: (1) the believer's union with Christ, the source of Christian holiness, and (2) moral behavior, a consequence of that union. This confusion and inversion is built on at least three faulty theological beliefs.

The first is the idea that if one does the right things (and, perhaps more important, if one does not do the wrong things), then one can produce and cultivate a relationship with Jesus Christ. Such a position is in clear contradiction to the classic Protestant doctrine that humans are in relationship with Christ by grace alone (*sola gratia*) and through faith alone (*sola fide*). In its place, legalism unwittingly developed a theology of "salvation by works," the view that a particular way of behaving is the cause of one's union with Christ.

Second, legalism is built on the faulty assumption that behavior modification is the primary goal of Christian holiness. Practically speaking, legalism acts as though the chief aim of holiness is an improvement in the way people conduct themselves. Undoubtedly, the Christian faith values, desires, and even works toward an improvement in the way people behave, but such behavior modification is not the ultimate purpose or goal of holiness. Instead, improved behavior is but a consequence of something more fundamental—the indwelling of Christ.

Third, legalism is built on the faulty belief that humans possess the ability to engage in right behaviors prior to and apart from being saved. If proper behavior is thought to result in relationship with Christ (rather than the other way around), then it necessarily follows that humans have the innate capacity to behave in that way. This view runs contrary to the teaching of Scripture, which, as we saw in previous chapters, speaks not about humans' innate moral abilities but about their fallenness, inability, and depravity.

License

Many who were raised within legalism's culture of strict and often ill-conceived restrictions have found the movement distasteful, spiritually vacuous, theologically misguided, and thus ill-fitting. Rather than rejecting the Christian faith outright, many have opted for a far more tolerant posture. Where legalism's response to most questions of morality is an almost automatic *No!*, this group's response to those same questions is an almost automatic *Why not?* Where legalism's posture is restrictive, this group's approach is open. In contrast to *legalism*, this group is characterized by *license*.

While this approach may seem far more palatable to many both inside and outside the church, it also suffers from significant theological confusion. First, while it correctly asserts that right behavior does not result in salvation, it practically suggests that there exists no relation between the two at all. Such a position is simply not scripturally tenable. The biblical injunctions to strive, struggle, and persevere in one's Christian walk are plentiful (e.g., Phil. 2:12; 1 Tim. 4:7–11; 2 Pet. 1:5–11). Paul describes this connection in a striking way in his letter to the Ephesians: "For it is by grace you have been saved, through faith—and this is not from yourselves, it is the gift of God—not by works, so that no one can boast. For we are God's handiwork, created in Christ Jesus to do good works, which God prepared in advance for us to do" (Eph. 2:8–10). This passage is particularly illuminating since we find within it emphases on both the gracious nature of God's saving work and humanity's responsibility to live a certain way. While the relationship between holiness and salvation is not one of cause and effect, as legalism seems to

127

suggest, there nevertheless is a clear link between the two. A particular kind of behavior does not result in salvation, but salvation does result in a particular kind of behavior.

Second, while the license approach may grant that holiness is God's desire for humanity, it acts as though holiness is something that is reserved for the afterlife or granted at the end of time. Rather than viewing holiness in terms of a process, which includes striving and discipline, the license approach views it as an instantaneous by-product of humanity's glorification that will result from God's gracious work alone. Such a position effectively discourages any interest in the pursuit of holiness in the present age. If one cannot achieve any significant progression in holiness in this life—and if God will grant it instantaneously in the life to come—why would one even try?

Liberty

The proper Christian posture in regard to the relation of salvation and holiness, of course, is neither legalism nor license. Too often the reaction to the spiritually abusive culture of legalism is to run to the spiritually vapid culture of license. While the latter group's critique of legalism may be spot-on, its proposed solution is without warrant. As in all things, *abusus non tollit usum* (abuse does not preclude proper use). The right response to legalism's skewed view of the relation between salvation and holiness is not, as in license, to deny that any relation exists. It is instead to understand what Scripture teaches about the proper relation—what we might call (for the sake of alliteration) *liberty*. Liberty affirms that salvation is fundamentally and completely a work of God's free grace bestowed apart from and even in spite of human behavior. Given humanity's desperate condition, humanity has nothing to offer in exchange for its salvation. At the same time, liberty affirms that salvation, behavior, and moral transformation are related. It recognizes that while behavior and moral transformation do not produce salvation, they are among salvation's intended consequences. Finally, liberty affirms that the object of salvation is more than moral transformation or behavior modification but encompasses a profound renovation or renewal of human nature.

At first blush the liberty (or freedom) view might seem similar to the license view, but the differences between the two are profound. While Christian notions of freedom are expressed in a variety of ways, the one thing that they cannot mean is the choice to sin. Biblically speaking, to sin is never to be free.[30] This is because sin results in freedom's very opposite: it makes one a slave (John 8:34). Moreover, freedom must not be understood as the ability or right to choose from an unrestricted range of options. Freedom is not the capricious or arbitrary exercise of the will. The idea that we can simply do anything we want to do is illusory.[31] Instead, freedom is always viewed in relation to a particular goal; it is the unrestricted opportunity to become everything that humanity was created to be.[32] As we saw in chapter 4, the central teaching of Scripture in regard to humanity is that it was formally created in the *imago dei* and was to continue to mature into the material *imago dei*. Since sin diminishes the *imago dei*, it is preposterous to view sin as a form of freedom. That which diminishes the image of God and thereby the human being can never be considered to be freedom; it can be considered only a form of slavery. Freedom is to be in intimate relation with God, to "will and to do his good pleasure" (Phil. 2:13), and to exist in his image.[33] True freedom is not a threat to the image of God but is instead "the renewal of the image of God in us."[34]

129

7

Holiness and the Nature and Goal of the Church

Before graduating high school, I landed a full-time job as a DJ at the highest-rated radio station in the area, where I got paid to do what I loved (and still love) to do: play and listen to popular music. Though I always had a keen interest in Top 40 music, this opportunity transported me from the ranks of the amateurs to that of the professionals (and made me the envy of a number of my high school peers). As a result of having spent untold hours in front of a microphone and behind the speakers, I can still name the song title and artist of hundreds of songs simply by hearing the opening note or two. This is true for both mainstream hits and more marginal or regional ones. One of the latter came from a blue-collar Canadian rock band, the Northern Pikes (named after the carnivorous fish that cruises the lakes of the northern hemisphere). While the band had a number of songs that did quite well in Canada in the late 1980s and early 1990s, their most commercially successful song—hitting number six in Canada and even cracking the Top 100 in the United States when it came out in 1990—told the story of an average-looking young man who met, dated, and fell in love with a stunningly beautiful woman, who turned out to be more attractive outwardly than inwardly. The title (and recurring hook) of the song says it all: "She Ain't Pretty, She Just Looks That Way."

When it comes to the holiness of the church, the exact opposite is the case. Though it may look far from beautiful on the surface, the church is holy. Indeed, "holy" is one of the four historic marks, or attributes, of the church—alongside "one," "catholic," and "apostolic." This perspective goes back in history almost to the time of the institution's very founding. Ignatius of Antioch (35–107), who is thought to be a disciple of the apostle John, used such language to describe the nature of the church.[1] Later, the Nicene-Constantinopolitan Creed (381) referred to the church in this way as well. While so much of Christian doctrine has changed over the past two thousand years, this tenet of the faith continues to be affirmed each week in innumerable congregations around the world.

Still, one need not look very far to find all sorts of reasons to reject the church's self-designation of holiness as disingenuous, misdirected, or just plain delusional. The church has a long list of skeletons in its closet, and books on church history are chock-full of crises, errors, sins, and schisms. At various times and in various places, the church has not only condoned but actively promoted and participated in war, slavery, exploitation, oppression, and cultural genocide. The church has even provided biblical and theological justification for many of these heinous practices. Even in recent history, it has allowed itself to be co-opted by those with unholy schemes, as when the German state church capitulated to the Nazi regime in the early to mid-twentieth century. And it has envisioned and engaged in particularly diabolical systems and practices, as when Canadian churches developed, promoted, and administered the Canadian Indian residential school system.[2] Yet in the face of all of this apparent and even blatant unholiness, the church has continued to confess its holiness!

The question of this chapter is how we might affirm this tenet of the Christian faith and confess this section of its creed in light of all the obvious and overwhelming evidence to the contrary. Building on our discussion of holiness from the previous chapters, I argue that we can continue to affirm the church's holiness only when we understand the true source and nature of that holiness. The church's holiness, like the holiness of all created things, is never its own by nature. While the church's holiness is real, it is not self-constituted, self-sustained, or grounded in itself or its actions. Rather, the holiness of the church, like the holiness of any created thing, is a derived holiness, a second-order holiness, an ever-dependent holiness, a holiness that comes from God and is proper to him alone. And just as we defined God's holiness primarily in terms of God's transcendence and only secondarily in terms of God's moral perfection, so too the church's holiness is found first in its otherness as having been indwelt by God and only secondarily in its actions.

The Otherness of the Church

Throughout this book, I have repeatedly noted that creaturely holiness is always derived from and dependent on the creature's ongoing relation to God. The same is true in regard to the church: the church's holiness is grounded in its relation to

God, the Holy One. Methodist theologian Thomas Oden sums up this idea concisely: "The church is holy because her Lord is holy."[3] Likewise, Presbyterian theologian Edmund Clowney writes: "Because they belong to the separated One, his people are separate."[4] The source of the church's holiness is ever and always "because she belongs to the Triune God."[5] Scripture uses numerous metaphors to describe the church, yet almost without exception they denote the essential place that the church's relation to God has in its own identity: the people of God, the body of Christ, the temple of the Holy Spirit. The church is not just a people; it is the people *of God*. It is not merely a body; it is the body *of Christ*. It is not merely a temple; it is the temple *of the Holy Spirit*. Without the relation, the metaphors lose the heart of their meaning. The church's relation to the Triune God distinguishes it from all other groups, societies, and organizations. The church's distinct and basic relation to God makes it the *communio sanctorum*—the holy community. Indeed, the church's relation to God is what makes it the church. This can be seen in the way the church is described in relation to each person of the Trinity.

The People of God

Just as God is the one who created "the heavens and the earth" out of nothing (Ps. 33:6; John 1:3; Rom. 4:17; Heb. 11:3; 2 Pet. 3:5), so too is he solely responsible for the creation of the church. The church owes its very existence to him. Fundamentally, the church is not a product of human will, ingenuity, or effort. While we often think of the church as a human creation, the church owes its very existence to the initiative, grace, work, and presence of the Triune God alone. It was elected by the Father, was reconciled by the Son, and is being perfected by the Holy Spirit.

As the people of God, the church finds its origin in God's selection and calling of Abraham (Gen. 12:1–3) and even more so in the covenant that God made with Israel while it was still captive in Egypt. In speaking to the people through Moses, God said, "I will take you as my own people and I will be your God" (Exod. 6:7).[6] In the New Testament, the church is described as having been grafted into Israel and, as a result, included in the covenant that God has made with her (Rom. 11:11–24). It is by the will and the choice of the sovereign Father that these people, who were once not a people, are now *God's* people (Eph. 1:3–6; 1 Pet. 1:2). Election by the Father is what defines them as a people. It is not their ethnicity, history, or religious practice. What distinguishes them as God's people is their having been chosen by him. While everything owes its existence to God, the church is composed of those who have been elected by the Father. It is the *ecclesia*, the *called ones*.

The holiness of the church is found not only in its being created *by* God but also in its being created *for* him. While all humanity was created to "glorify God, and to enjoy him forever,"[7] only the church has as its *mission* to do so. And this is not merely the church's task or privilege but its raison d'être, its very purpose for existence (Matt. 22:37; Mark 12:30; Luke 10:27; 1 Cor. 10:13; 1 John 2–4).

The holiness of the church also rests in its open recognition of God's rightful reign. God is certainly "Lord of all" (Rom. 10:12), but the church alone recognizes, respects, and submits to God's rightful role as sovereign. Consequently, the church alone can respond to God and his rule properly. Recognizing who God is and all that he has done for them, those who make up the church cannot help but respond in thanksgiving and praise (Eph. 1:15–16; 5:15–20; Col. 3:15; 1 Thess. 5:18; Rev.

7:9–12; 11:17). The ultimate task of a holy people is to respond appropriately to a holy God.[8]

The church's thanksgiving and worship are not limited to its words but are expressed in its mission. Here too the church's holiness is evident. The church is distinguished from all other groups in that it is God's active agent of redemption in the world. The church alone has been commissioned by Christ to evangelize the world and to be God's colaborer in the expansion of his kingdom (Matt. 28:19–20; Luke 24:47; Acts 1:8; 1 Cor. 3:9; 2 Cor. 6:1). The church alone has been entrusted with the ministry of the Word (John 14:3), and it alone has been given the keys to the kingdom of heaven (Matt. 16:19; 18:18; John 20:23). For that reason, the church has long held to the bold and exclusive claim made by third-century church father Cyprian: *extra ecclesiam nulla salus*, there is no salvation outside the church. While this phrase has been interpreted in many ways, it affirms the basic truth that the church has been commissioned by God as the ongoing agent of his saving work in the world.[9] As John Webster writes of the members of the church, "If we are elected to holiness, then we have been extracted from the sphere of human autonomy."[10] In other words, the church's mission is not the product of its own ingenuity, a realization of its own need or giftedness, or the result of an analysis of market trends or needs. The church has been freed from the frustration and burden of self-determination. Its mission comes from God himself and is, therefore, holy.

The Body of Christ

While the Father's work of election is fundamental to the church's holiness, it does not stand alone. The church's holiness is also a product of the reconciling ministry of the Son

(2 Cor. 5:18). The church is not only the elect people of God; it is also the body of Christ, "a community of people who are reconciled to God and to one another."[11] The Son has redeemed them, reconciled them to God, and thereby made them holy (Gal. 4:5; Eph. 1:7; Col. 1:18–20). While the rest of humanity is not yet reconciled to him but remains hostile (Rom. 8:7), those who compose the church are alone called God's "friends" (John 15:13–14; James 2:23) and even the "bride" that Christ loves and gave up his life for (Eph. 5:25). The aim of the Son's reconciling work is to cleanse the church's members from the stain of sin (Col. 1:22) and to free them from power of sin (Titus 2:14) so that the church might truly be the body of Christ in the world (1 Cor. 12:12–31).

One of the ways that the New Testament expresses the relationship between Christ and the church is through the language of being "in Christ." To be "in Christ" is a central and recurring theme in the New Testament and a favorite phrase of the apostle Paul. It appears in every one of his epistles, except for Titus, and is used in some form no fewer than 165 times throughout his letters. Being "in Christ" is the church's sine qua non; being "in Christ" is essential to its nature. Colin Gunton writes that the church "is distinguished by one feature: its relation to the Jesus proclaimed in the message of the gospel."[12] Being "in Christ" is even more fundamental to the church than the four marks of the church we discussed above: one, holy, catholic, apostolic. Those marks are expressions and consequences of being "in Christ." The church is *one* because its Lord is one. The church is *holy* because its Lord is holy. The church is *catholic* because no one comes to the Father but by the Son who indwells it (Matt. 28:19–20; John 14:6; Acts 1:8). The church is *apostolic* because the Christ who indwells it has commissioned it and is the source of its testimony (John 3:16–17; 7:16–18, 29; 8:24; 20:21–22; 1 Cor. 11:23; 15:3; Gal. 4:4; 1 Tim. 6:3).

Being "in Christ" makes the church holy. The church is holy because it is actually, mysteriously, indwelt by Christ himself. The church's relation to Christ is not at arm's length but is so intimate that Paul describes the church as Christ's body. As a result, even in spite of contemporary appearances, the church is holy. Its holiness, we might say, is objective. As Edmund Clowney writes, the church is holy "not just ideally, but actually, because it is composed of a people who are united to Jesus Christ."[13] Perhaps this is what Paul was referring to when he wrote, "It is because of [God] that you are in Christ Jesus, who has become for us wisdom from God—that is, our righteousness, holiness, and redemption" (1 Cor. 1:30). Holiness is not a commodity or property that Christ gives to the church. Christ himself is the church's holiness. The presence of Christ within the church makes the church the holy body of Christ.

The Temple of the Holy Spirit

As a work of the Triune God, the holiness of the church is, therefore, also a result of the work of the Holy Spirit. As Craig Van Gelder writes, when Scripture calls the church holy, it "speaks most directly to the reality that the church is a creation of the Spirit."[14] Jesus taught his disciples that the work of the Holy Spirit would lead the church "into all truth" (John 16:13). While the work of the Spirit moves more widely than solely within the church, the Spirit works in the church in a number of distinct ways. Among other things, the Spirit *regenerates* the church (John 3:5–8; Titus 3:5), *leads* the church (Matt. 4:1; Luke 4:1; Rom. 8:14; Gal. 5:18), *empowers* the church (Luke 4:14; 24:49; Acts 1:8; Rom. 15:19), *intercedes* for the church

(Rom. 8:26), *reveals* to the church what it has received from God (1 Cor. 2:12), *helps* the church to understand the deep things of God (1 Cor. 2:10), and *transforms* the church into the image of Christ (2 Cor. 3:18).

One of the images used in the New Testament to describe the relationship between the Holy Spirit and the church is the temple. The first-century Jews were well-acquainted with the temple. They knew well what it looked like, smelled like, and sounded like. They knew well what kind of things went on there and, just as certainly, which things should not. Undoubtedly, for many of the first-century Jews, those images, smells, sounds, and activities were what made the temple holy and distinguished that place from any other. Such a perspective and understanding is reasonable, and we might be tempted to assume the same. Yet, while each of these characteristics of the temple had its place, none of them made the temple holy—not even the altar of sacrifice, the bronze basin, the holy place, the holy of holies, the ark of the covenant, or the mercy seat. That which made the temple holy—indeed that which made the temple *the temple*—was nothing other than the presence of the Spirit of God. Apart from the Spirit's presence, it was just a building.[15]

Paul must have had this understanding in mind when he called the church the temple of the Holy Spirit (1 Cor. 6:19; cf. 1 Cor. 3:16, 17; 2 Cor. 6:16). The church is the temple because, from the day of Pentecost, it is where the Spirit of God has taken up residence. When Paul calls the church the temple, he isn't just a employing a figure of speech or making a comparison. Since "temple" refers not to a building but to a place (any place) where the Spirit of God resides, the church can be truly called "the temple."

Today the very mention of the word "church" evokes particular images among many. For some, those images are of rising
stone edifices with arched windows, stained glass, and a steeple.
For others, those images include the performance of certain
rites such as weddings, baptisms, or funerals. Still others may
recall the rhetoric of a fiery preacher or the vibrant tones of a
pristinely robed choir. For many people, the presence of those
kinds of things is what makes church the church. Yet as with
the temple, so the church is defined not by those things but by
the presence of the Spirit in its midst.

In sum, the church is holy not because of what it does or how
it appears on the outside but because of its special relationship
to the Triune God. This means that the church's holiness is, in
a sense, an alien holiness. The holiness of the church is not a
product of the people who constitute it. It is not self-generated,
self-constituted, or self-acquired. Rather, it is the result of God
electing the church as his people, Christ commissioning the
church as his body, and the Holy Spirit indwelling the church as
a temple. In this way the church is holy even when its members
continue to sin. Yet, as we will see in the next section, God's
goal and design for the church is that its actions will reflect its
true nature.

The Morality of the Church

We saw in the previous section that the church's holiness is
fundamentally grounded in its relationship to the Triune God.
Ultimately, though, God's purpose for the church is that it would
reflect the character of God in all that it does. The holiness of
the church is grounded in a particular kind of relationship,
and that relationship cannot help but affect the way the church

conducts itself. The will of God is that the church be exemplary and excellent in regard to its conduct. The call of God is "to a holy life" (2 Tim. 1:9). There is thus a necessary moral or ethical dimension to the church's holiness. God's desire and intention for the church is that it should be blameless. In writing to the Thessalonians, Paul makes this clear: "It is God's will that you should be sanctified" (1 Thess. 4:3). In this passage, the term "sanctified" is referring to the church's behavior and not just its status.[16] Unlike the world, the church is to "live in order to please God" (1 Thess. 4:1). Though holiness is grounded in the church's relationship to God, this relationship is to result in a particular way of life.

The moral and ethical dimension of holiness is beyond the ability of the church, left to its own devices, to attain. The ability to live blamelessly is not something that the church possesses independently. It comes only by the indwelling and leading of the Spirit of God. The Holy Spirit enables the church to attain what God has called it to, empowering it to confess Christ (1 Cor. 12:3), to "put to death the misdeeds of the body" (Rom. 8:13), and "to be obedient to Jesus Christ" (1 Pet. 1:2). The task of the church in regard to morality, then, is not to strike out on its own with the best of intentions and a firm resolve. Instead, humbly, it is to call on God for the grace to be and to do what he has created it for. As sixteenth-century Reformer John Calvin—who was by no means a proponent of moral laxity—noted, the church's holiness is seen in the very fact that its morality is advancing, even though it is not yet perfect or complete.[17]

This "already but not yet" aspect of the church's holiness entails that its actions must always be rooted in its confession of faith and its confession of sin. Over its history, the church has developed a number of summaries, or "confessions," of its faith (e.g., the Augsburg Confession, the Belgic Confession, the Westminster Confession). At the heart of such confessions is a declaration of God's existence, nature, and relation to creation. The church acknowledges that God exists and that he exists as the Trinity: Father, Son, and Holy Spirit. Moreover, the church confesses its complete and utter dependence on this God for its existence and for its holiness.[18] Having confessed who God is and what his holy nature entails, the church is then able to recognize and confess its sin as well. In so doing, the church acknowledges that it is not yet what God desires it to be. The process of sanctification begins with the church's admission of its sins. Only then can the church begin to turn from sin and pursue what God has called it to be: "holy and blameless" (Eph. 5:27).

EXCURSUS: **Holiness and the Donatist Heresy**

In chapters 2 and 3, I noted that, when it comes to discussions on holiness, the temptation to turn to heresy is real. This is because certain heresies suggest that Jesus's humanity is fundamentally different than our own and, as a result, we cannot be held to his example. We turn to these heresies in an attempt to let ourselves off the hook, to shirk our responsibility to live holy lives. These previously discussed heresies, however, are not the only ones that may tempt us when we consider the nature and practice of Christian holiness. There is another that is easy to fall prey to: Donatism.

In the fourth century, the church in North Africa faced the threats of both persecution from the Roman authorities and internal divisions resulting from those persecutions. There, a group who would become known as the Donatists were tearing the fragile unity of the church apart through their obsession with the purity of the church in the face and aftermath of persecution. The Donatists taught that since the church is fundamentally holy, it can be composed only of those without sin, and, just as controversially, that should a priest have personal sin, his ministry is automatically rendered ineffective and his leadership illegitimate. Consequently, the Donatists asserted that since they alone had proved to be righteous in the face of persecution, they alone were members of the true church and only the ministry of their priests was effective. Donatism was declared heretical by the Synod of Arles in 314, a decision that was later upheld by Emperor Constantine. Yet in spite of its being condemned by both church and state, Donatism would survive in North Africa until the Islamic conquest of that area in the seventh century.[19]

One might be tempted to admire the unswerving and uncompromising dedication of the Donatists. They certainly took seriously Peter's call to "make every effort to be found spotless [and] blameless" (2 Pet. 3:14). Yet the Donatists suffered from significant biblical and theological difficulties in their understanding of holiness and its relation to the church.

First, while holiness is one of the historic marks of the church, we have seen that there are others as well. Donatists challenged at least one of the other marks: catholicism. To talk about the church being catholic is to affirm that it is made up of a variety of people—all nations, races, and ages—and not just one. But it is also to affirm that the church includes people of varied spiritual maturity. While Donatism was deeply concerned with promoting and maintaining the holiness of the church, it denied God's call to catholicity. Many Christians need spiritual growth and maturity, yet they remain members of the church. For Donatism, the only church that exists is the ideal church, the church that is everything that God intends it to be. Scripture, however, speaks of the church in both its ideal and its present form. The ideal church is "without stain or wrinkle or any other blemish, but holy and blameless" (Eph. 5:27). It is the church that God is making and perfecting until it will be revealed in the last days. The present church is that community in which sin continues to be found, even among the leadership (1 Tim. 5:20). This distinction between the ideal and the present reality of the church is made within the same letter. Paul addresses the church in Ephesus as "God's holy people" (Eph. 1:1), suggesting that holiness is something they already possess; yet, a little while later, he calls this same group to pursue holiness, suggesting that in some way they do not yet possess it (Eph. 4:12–13). The Ephesians, it seems, were both already holy and still yet to be made holy. Thus while it may be tempting to assert that only the ideal church is the true church, Scripture does not allow us that luxury. It refers to both the ideal and the present reality as the church. We must hold both understandings of the church in tension. The church is both presently holy and—as God enables it—progressing toward holiness.

Second, and related to the first, Donatism's very definition of holiness was problematic. Donatism erred by understanding holiness primarily—if not exclusively—as a moral category, almost entirely ignoring holiness as the gracious consequence of the church's unique relationship with God. For Donatists, holiness was about behavior, full stop. But as we have seen in this chapter, while moral purity is something after which the church is to strive, the church's holiness refers more fundamentally to its relationship with and dependence on God. The church is holy first and foremost because of its relationship to the Father, Son, and Holy Spirit.

Third, Donatism's definition of holiness tended to be self-centered and self-congratulatory. For the Donatists, to be truly holy was to be Donatist. Effectively, they held themselves up as the standard of holiness. In doing so, they not only denied Christ's proper role as that standard but also overestimated their own moral purity. They practically considered themselves to be without sin, thus denying John's teaching that those who profess to be without sin "deceive [themselves] and the truth is not in [them]" (1 John 1:8).

Finally, Donatism effectively denied the effectiveness, sovereignty, and sufficiency of the grace of God. Donatists located the source and effectiveness of Christian ministry in the moral character of the priest. If the priests were fit, then the ministry that they produced would be effective. If they were not fit, then the ministry that they produced would not be effective. North African theologian and church father Augustine (354–430) built his great reputation in part by opposing Donatism and arguing that the effectiveness of Christian ministry is grounded neither in the character nor in the ability of the human minister. Instead, all Christian ministry is grounded in the grace of God. Christian ministry is never about the construction of grace but is about the communication of grace already secured. While the minister has a vital role to play, that role is instrumental. Christ himself is the true minister; he is the one who has provided for and extends salvation. All other so-called ministers are but his vicars, representatives of Christ who communicate to others the grace that Christ alone has already secured. The character and abilities of a given minister may enhance or detract from the communication of God's grace, but they do not determine its effectiveness.

The Donatist movement died out well over one thousand years ago, but the heretical spirit that gave birth to Donatism is alive and well within some pockets of contemporary evangelicalism. One can still find those who distort the church's rightful concern with holiness into a stance of separation and isolation from Christians who worship or think differently from them, thus effectively denying both the unity and catholicity of the church universal. One can still find people who view holiness as an exclusively moral category and who hold themselves up as the standard to which all Christians must conform, thus denying Christ's role as the model and source of human holiness. And, finally, one can find those who continue to reject the validity of other denominations and churches whose ministers don't conform to their own practices, thus denying the sufficiency of God's grace to work even through flawed individuals. In spite of the most honorable of intentions, heresy can never be the avenue to holiness. In fact, to entertain heresy—any heresy—in the interest of holiness is a devilish monstrosity.

Conclusion

In the preface I mentioned that this book is written out of the conviction that we must first understand holiness as a theological category (the what-is) if we hope to properly pursue holiness in our lives (the how-to). After describing our culture's current desire and need for holiness (chap. 1), I attempted to define holiness in a way that is faithful to Scripture (chap. 2) and the Christian theological tradition (chap. 3) before showing how this definition of holiness relates to our understanding of humanity (chap. 4), sin (chap. 5), salvation (chap. 6), and the church (chap. 7). I want to conclude by briefly reiterating four key points that I believe should provide the foundation for any proper theological understanding of holiness and thus for any proper pursuit of holiness in one's life.

The first point emphasized throughout the book is that *holiness is not merely a matter of behavior but is fundamentally a way of being.* At its very essence, holiness describes a type of existence. To be holy is to be transcendent, wholly other, fundamentally distinct, absolutely unique. Contrary to how it is so often understood, holiness is not primarily a moral or ethical category.

Unfortunately, understanding holiness as a way of being has been forgotten by many evangelicals, including many who are from the Holiness traditions. The overwhelming tendency is to understand holiness as a matter of what we do (or don't do). As I have argued throughout the book, such a view of holiness is incomplete at best and erroneous at worst. If one is to effectively pursue or attain holiness, this common understanding must be revised and corrected. Those who wish to pursue holiness must seek not only to reform their behavior but even more fundamentally to become something other than what they were before. This is not to suggest that holiness has nothing to do with behavior, but it is to say that holiness as a way of behaving can never be divorced from holiness as a way of being. Any pursuit of holiness, therefore, must start with the pursuit of a relationship with God, the Holy One, and only then consider how one's conduct flows out of that relationship.

This first point dovetails nicely with the second point emphasized throughout the book: *true holiness is a divine property alone*. Only God is truly holy. As the classic hymn "Holy, Holy, Holy" says in reference to God: "Only thou art holy; there is none beside thee."[1] God alone is absolutely unique; he alone transcends everything else; he alone is wholly other; he alone is *qdš*. Everything else is created; everything else is common, or *ḥōl*.

Holiness extends both to the way God exists and to the way he acts. As we saw in chapter 3, nothing else exists in the same way God does. Nothing else has aseity. Nothing else is absolutely free. Nothing else is eternal. Moreover, only God's actions are always and uncompromisingly righteous, pure, and flawless. In

God, these two aspects of holiness—transcendence and moral perfection—are indissolubly linked. And this is not merely coincidental, as each are expressions of the singular holiness of God. Remembering that God's holiness applies equally and necessarily to his way of being *and* acting reinforces our first point that our view of human holiness cannot be truncated to include moral considerations alone.

A necessary corollary of our second point is a third: *all forms of creaturely holiness are derived from and constantly dependent on God*. Since holiness is an essential property of God alone, it follows that nothing else is essentially holy. Yet, as we saw in chapter 2, Scripture describes a variety of created things as holy. Unlike the holiness of God, however, the holiness of such created things—days, ground, the tabernacle, people—is always inextricably dependent on their relation to God by God's grace. The holiness of all other things, including humanity, is real, but only as a derived and dependent holiness. Such dependent holiness is never self-constituted, self-achieved, or self-contained. The holiness of such things is never intrinsic to their nature but is always and constantly grounded in their dynamic relation to God, the Holy One. Such things are holy not in virtue of any merit of individual achievement but only by God's grace.

As we saw in chapter 4, this is the case even for human holiness. In all of its aspects and expressions, human holiness is always derived from and dependent on its relation to the Holy One. We saw that even in the manner of humanity's creation in the *imago dei*, humans are set apart from the rest of creation by the gracious act of God. Again, holiness is a real feature of humanity, but it is so only as humans reflect God's image formally and materially. When this occurs, the human mysteriously partakes of the divine nature—and thus is graced to be able to

149

partake of holiness itself. Ultimately, human holiness is the result of the gracious gift of God and not of human achievement. As such, any human pursuit of holiness must be motivated not by desire to live up to a moral code but by the desire for a union with God. This leads us directly to our final point.

Fourth, we have seen that *human holiness is grounded in union with Christ by the power of the Holy Spirit*. Holiness is not a discrete commodity. It is not a property. It is not a "thing." Holiness as such has no existence of its own. Instead, holiness is a way to describe the manner of God's existence. Therefore, if humanity is to be holy, it will not be the result of its reception of some commodity, property, or "thing," even if that should come from God. Instead, human holiness can come about only as the human is brought into an intimate relation to the One who is holy. The relation that makes human holiness possible is described in Scripture as being "in Christ" and in Christian theology as "union with Christ." This union is the necessary and exclusive means of human holiness in its fullest sense.

As we have seen, Jesus is the means of human holiness in terms of both being and behaving. In the first case, because of the indwelling of Christ by the power of the Holy Spirit, the believer truly, though mysteriously, participates in the holy nature of the divine. In the second case, it is only through union with Christ, the one who is without sin (Heb. 4:15), that humans are able to overcome their propensity to sin and to pursue godly behavior. Thus, once again, anyone in pursuit of holiness must keep in mind that holiness is fundamentally dependent on the believer's union with Christ. It must move beyond merely prescribing various "dos" and "don'ts" and focus instead on those attitudes, disciplines, and habits that develop and deepen one's relationship with Christ.

This book started out by noting that we live in a time in which both the church and the world, in numerous and various ways, demonstrate a desire and a need for holiness. The church and its members would thus do well to seize the opportunity provided by this current climate of openness to profess, promote, and pursue holiness. No matter the technique or approach (the how-to) that the church employs in its pursuit, I would suggest that it must start with a proper theological understanding of what holiness is (and is not). My hope and prayer is that each of the four points discussed in this conclusion—as well as our discussion of holiness throughout the book—might serve as a solid theological foundation for that pursuit, as each one is a fundamental and integral aspect of a holistic Christian theology of holiness.

Notes

Chapter 1 The Desire and Need for Holiness

1. See Robert Webber, *Evangelicals on the Canterbury Trail: Why Evangelicals Are Attracted to the Liturgical Church* (Waco: Word, 1985); Webber, *The Younger Evangelicals: Facing the Challenges of the New World* (Grand Rapids: Baker Books, 2002). In the Ancient-Future series, the initial offering was Webber's *Ancient-Future Faith: Rethinking Evangelicalism for a Postmodern World* (Grand Rapids: Baker, 1999). This series also includes books on worship, evangelism, and the observance of the church year.

2. This series, which samples the commentary of various church fathers on the Scriptures, was launched in 1998 with the volume *Mark*, edited by Thomas C. Oden and Christopher A. Hall (Downers Grove, IL: InterVarsity, 1998). Since that time, the series has been translated into a number of languages and has spawned similar projects, including the Ancient Christian Doctrine series and the Reformation Commentary on Scripture (both published by IVP Academic).

3. D. James Kennedy and Thomas H. Stebbins, *Evangelism Explosion*, 4th ed. (Wheaton: Tyndale, 1996), 77. While the authors do not deny that there are present implications to salvation, the nature of the "Diagnostic Questions" they pose could lead one to believe that salvation is primarily, if not exclusively, a future event.

4. Not surprisingly, theological views on the nature of human being are not singular, whether one is arguing for a version of monism (the belief that human being is essentially an integrated whole) or a qualified dualism (the belief that humanity is composed of an interrelated body and a soul). See John W. Cooper, *Body, Soul, and Life Everlasting: Biblical Anthropology and the Monism-Dualism Debate*, rev. ed. (Grand Rapids: Eerdmans, 2000); Kevin J. Corcoran, *Rethinking Human Nature: A Christian Materialist Alternative to the Soul* (Grand Rapids:

Baker Academic, 2006); William Hasker, *The Emergent Self* (Ithaca, NY: Cornell University Press, 1999); Nancey Murphy, *Bodies and Souls, or Spirited Bodies?* (New York: Cambridge University Press, 2006).

5. This is the answer to the first question, "What is the chief end of man?" of "The Shorter Catechism." See *The Confession of Faith: Together with The Larger Catechism and The Shorter Catechism with the Scripture Proofs*, 3rd ed. (Atlanta: Committee for Christian Education and Publications, 1990), 3.

6. Such an attitude has manifested itself repeatedly within the history of the Holiness-Pentecostal tradition. See Vinson Synan, *The Holiness-Pentecostal Tradition: Charismatic Movements in the Twentieth Century*, 2nd ed. (Grand Rapids: Eerdmans, 1997), 36, 40, 89.

7. Among those who describe Luther's relationship to this doctrine as a "rediscovery" is the widely influential Welsh minister of Westminster Chapel of London, D. Martyn Lloyd-Jones (1899–1981). See Martyn Lloyd-Jones, *Great Doctrines of the Bible*, vol. 1, *God the Holy Spirit* (Wheaton: Crossway, 1997), 167.

8. More information on these two groups may be found at www.redletterchristians.org and www.holinessandunity.org.

9. Larry D. Hart, e.g., boldly proclaims: "We cannot understand the church apart from Christ, nor can we fully understand Christ apart from the church!" See Larry D. Hart, *Truth Aflame: Theology for the Church in Renewal*, rev. ed. (Grand Rapids: Zondervan, 2005), 286–87.

10. Among the many groups attempting to undertake this kind of "holistic" work in the United States is Evangelicals for Social Action at the Sider Center of Eastern University (www.evangelicalsforsocialaction.org).

11. Augustine, *Confessions*, trans. R. S. Pine-Coffin (New York: Penguin, 1961), 21.

12. Rudolf Otto, *The Idea of the Holy*, 2nd ed., trans. John W. Harvey (New York: Oxford University Press, 1958).

13. William Paul Young, *The Shack: Where Tragedy Confronts Eternity* (Newbury Park, CA: Windblown, 2007).

14. In the last few years, the question of the true rate of Christian divorce has been debated both inside and outside the church. Whether one accepts the assertion that Christian divorce rates do not vary significantly from that of the rest of the population, the rate at which even conservative Christians are divorcing should be cause for concern. For examples of those on each side of this debate, see Bradley R. E. Wright, *Christians Are Hate-Filled Hypocrites . . . and Other Lies You've Been Told* (Bloomington, MN: Bethany House, 2010); Jennifer Glass and Philip Levchak, "Red States, Blue States, and Divorce: Understanding the Impact of Conservative Protestantism on Regional Variation in Divorce Rates," *American Journal of Sociology* 119, no. 4, (January 2014): 1002–46.

15. H. C. G. Moule, *Thoughts on Christian Sanctity* (London: Seeley, 1885), 9.

16. Jerry Bridges, *The Pursuit of Holiness* (Colorado Springs: NavPress, 2006), 11.

17. Even among those denominations for whom holiness remains a central focus, there is no unanimity either on what holiness refers to or on how it may be successfully pursued or attained. This is clearly seen in the various books that have been written on the topic that, rather than showing how these various traditions agree, focus on how they differ. Two of the most notable books are Melvin E. Dieter et al., *Five Views on Sanctification*, rev. ed. (Grand Rapids: Zondervan, 1996); and Donald L. Alexander, ed., *Christian Spirituality: Five Views of Sanctification* (Downers Grove, IL: IVP Academic, 1988).

18. Thomas J. Oord and Michael Lodahl, *Relational Holiness: Responding to the Call of Love* (Kansas City, MO: Beacon Hill, 2005), 29–30.

19. There may be no clearer example of this kind of infighting than that of Harry Ironside's attack on his own Holiness movement roots in his polemically titled book *Holiness: The False and the True* (Neptune, NJ: Loizeaux, 1912).

Chapter 2 A Biblical Definition of Holiness

1. *The Princess Bride*, directed by Rob Reiner (1987; Beverly Hills, CA: MGM Home Entertainment, 2014), DVD.

2. The sections "The Ancient Near East" and "Ancient Israel" are built on the work of Donald L. Alexander, *The Pursuit of Godliness: Sanctification in Christological Perspective* (Lanham, MD: University Press of America, 1999), 26.

3. Alexander, *Pursuit of Godliness*, 26.

4. J. Muilenburg, "Holiness," in *The Interpreter's Dictionary of the Bible: An Illustrated Encyclopedia*, ed. George Arthur Buttrick (Nashville: Abingdon, 1962), 2:616–25.

5. Alexander, *Pursuit of Godliness*, 21.

6. Ibid., 21.

7. Ibid., 26; J. Muilenburg, "Holiness."

8. Alexander, *Pursuit of Godliness*, 22.

9. Ibid., 25–26; Baruch A. Levine, "The Language of Holiness: Perception of the Sacred in the Hebrew Bible," in *Backgrounds for the Bible*, ed. Michael Patrick O'Connor and David Noel Freedman (Winona Lake, IN: Eisenbrauns, 1987), 242.

10. Alexander, *Pursuit of Godliness*, 28.

11. For more on the Egyptians' treatment of Pharaoh as a deity, see "Pharaoh," in *Routledge Encyclopedia of Ancient Mediterranean Religions*, ed. Eric Orrin (Oxford: Routledge, 2015), 714; David Kinsley, *Goddesses' Mirror: The Visions of the Divine from East and West* (Albany, NY: SUNY Press, 1989), 165–70.

12. Alexander, *Pursuit of Godliness*, 34–35.

13. The sections "The Greco-Roman World" and "First-Century Judaism" are built on the work of Kent Brower, *Holiness in the Gospels* (Kansas City, MO: Beacon Hill, 2005).

14. Brower, *Holiness in the Gospels*, 21–22.

15. Ibid., 22–23.

16. Ibid., 24.

17. Ibid., 26.

18. For a more detailed treatment of these and other groups, see Donald E. Gowan, *Bridge between the Testaments: A Reappraisal of Judaism from the Exile to the Birth of Christianity*, 3rd rev. ed. (Allison Park, PA: Pickwick, 1986), 127–84.

19. Brower, *Holiness in the Gospels*, 26.

20. Walter C. Smith, "Immortal, Invisible, God Only Wise," in *Hymns of the Christian Life*, rev. ed. (Harrisburg, PA: Christian Publications, 1978), 15.

21. John H. Leith, ed., *Creeds of the Churches: A Reader in Christian Doctrine from the Bible to the Present*, 3rd ed. (Louisville: John Knox, 1982), 33.

22. For more on Docetism, Apollinarianism, and other heretical groups, see Justin S. Holcomb, *Know the Heretics* (Grand Rapids: Zondervan, 2014); and Ben Quash and Michael Ward, eds., *Heresies and How to Avoid Them: Why It Matters What Christians Believe* (Peabody, MA: Hendrickson, 2007).

23. Fred R. Shapiro, ed., *The Yale Book of Quotations* (New Haven: Yale University Press, 2006), 734.

24. For a more detailed treatment, see R. Albert Mohler Jr., "The Way the World Thinks: Meeting the Natural Mind in the Mirror and in the Marketplace," in *Thinking. Loving. Doing. A Call to Glorify God with Heart and Mind*, ed. John Piper and David Mathis (Wheaton: Crossway, 2011), 54–58; and Stephen K. Moroney, *The Noetic Effects of Sin: A Historical and Contemporary Exploration of How Sin Affects Our Thinking* (Lanham, MD: Lexington, 2000).

25. John Webster, *Holiness* (Grand Rapids: Eerdmans, 2003), 11.

26. Robert Robinson, "Come, Thou Fount," in *Hymns of the Christian Life*, 163.

Chapter 3 A Theological Investigation of Holiness

1. *Finding Nemo*, directed by Andrew Stanton and Lee Unkrich (Emeryville, CA: Pixar, 2003), DVD.

2. *The Oxford Dictionary of the Christian Church*, 3rd ed., ed. F. L. Cross and E. A. Livingstone (New York: Oxford University Press, 1997), defines "concupiscence" as follows: "In moral theology the inordinate desire for temporal ends which has its seat in the senses" (393).

3. As Donald Alexander writes, "One fact is indisputably clear: the pages of Old Testament Scripture abound with admonitions to holiness. The rationale undergirding these admonitions resides in the nature of Israel's God who is declared to be *holy* (Isa. 6:3; Ps. 89:18). Of all the attributes ascribed to be the divine nature, holiness by virtue of frequency and emphasis, occupies a position of singular importance. So dominant is this designation of God in the Old Testament and pre-eminent in its summons to the children of Israel that biblical scholars have characterized the entire religion of Israel as a *religion of holiness*" (*Pursuit of Godliness*, 19, emphasis original). See also Walther Eichrodt, *Theology of the Old Testament* (Philadelphia: Westminster, 1961), 1:270; J. Hanel, *Die Religion der Heiligkeit* (Gütersloh: Bertelmans, 1931), 27. According to Alexander, Hanel was one of the first to suggest that holiness was central to Israelite religion (*Pursuit of Godliness*, 54).

4. I'm borrowing this language from Allan Coppedge, who writes in *Portraits of God: A Biblical Theology of Holiness* (Downers Grove, IL: IVP Academic, 2001) that "God, who is holy, is in himself the standard of all holiness" (238). See also Kenneth A. Mathews, *Leviticus: Holy God, Holy People*, Preaching the Word (Wheaton: Crossway, 2009), 168; Henry T. Blackaby and Roy T. Edgemon, *The Ways of God: How God Reveals Himself before a Watching World* (Nashville: Broadman & Holman, 2000), 81.

5. As R. C. Sproul writes in *The Holiness of God* (Wheaton: Tyndale, 1985), "When the Bible calls God holy, it means primarily that God is transcendentally separate" (55).

6. In John Webster's essay "Life in and of Himself: Reflections on God's Aseity," in *Engaging the Doctrine of God: Contemporary Protestant Perspectives*, ed. Bruce L. McCormack (Grand Rapids: Baker Academic, 2008), he writes that aseity "indicates the glory and plenitude of the life of the Holy Trinity in its self-existent and self-moving originality, its underived fullness. In every respect, God is of Himself God" (107–8).

7. Webster notes that while the concept of aseity stands on its own as a description of God, it is also complementary to the essential contingency of the created order. See Webster, "Life in and of Himself," 108.

8. See Joseph Pohle, *God: His Knowability, Essence, and Attributes; A Dogmatic Treatise* (London: Aeterna, 2015).

9. In *The Doctrine of God in Reformed Orthodoxy, Karl Barth, and the Utrecht School: A Study in Method and Content* (Leiden: Brill, 2013), Dolf te Velde writes, "God's holiness means that God himself is the ultimate norm by which everything is measured and to which all God's actions are directed" (231). See also John Webster, *God without Measure: Working Papers in Christian Theology*, vol. 1, *God and the Works of God* (London: Bloomsbury, 2016), 191.

10. In *Christian Beliefs: Twenty Basics Every Christian Should Know* (Grand Rapids: Zondervan, 2005), Wayne Grudem observes, "Although different analogies from creation can help us a bit in understanding the Trinity, ultimately all analogies fail in describing this mystery, for they attempt to explain the being of God in terms of the creation. They are attempts to explain how God is like the creation. But nothing in creation is exactly like God's being" (39).

11. As te Velde writes, "Holiness is an essential property, proper to all three Persons in God" (*Doctrine of God*, 231).

12. On this point, see Eugene H. Merrill, *Everlasting Dominion: A Theology of the Old Testament* (Nashville: B&H, 2006), 59.

13. As Colin Gunton writes in *Act and Being: Toward a Theology of the Divine Attributes* (Grand Rapids: Eerdmans, 2003), "It is not a matter of what *we attribute*, but of what he *reveals himself* to be" (9, emphasis original).

14. E.g., Millard Erickson enumerates nineteen distinct attributes of God, and Wayne Grudem lists twenty. See Erickson, *Christian Theology*, 3rd ed. (Grand Rapids: Baker Academic, 2013), 233–313; Grudem, *Systematic Theology: An Introduction to Biblical Doctrine* (Grand Rapids: Zondervan, 1994), 186.

15. According to Alec Motyer, *Isaiah: An Introduction and Commentary* (Downers Grove, IL: InterVarsity, 1999), "Hebrew uses repetition to express either a superlative . . . or a totality. But here for the only time in the Hebrew Bible a quality is 'raised to the power of three,' as if to say that the divine holiness is so far beyond anything the human mind can grasp that a 'super-superlative' has to be invented to express it and, furthermore, that this transcendent holiness is the total truth about God" (71).

16. For a fuller examination of what is meant by the term "person" in regard to the nature of the Triune God, see Thomas C. Oden, *Systematic Theology*, vol. 1, *The Living God* (San Francisco: Harper & Row, 1987), 84–87; and William Hasker, "The Divine Three: What Is a 'Person'?," in *Metaphysics and the Tri-Personal God* (Oxford: Oxford University Press, 2013), 19–25.

17. As Oden writes, "The divine will is the infinite power of God to determine God's own intentions, execute actions, and use means adequate to the ends intended" (*Systematic Theology*, 1:90).

18. Oden notes that while other freedoms exist, including human freedom, they are always dependent on and granted by God's freedom. See Oden, *Systematic Theology*, 1:91–92. Most traditional theologians agree that God's desires and actions are always consistent with his good and perfect nature such that it would in a sense be *impossible* for him to act contrary to his nature. This is not typically viewed as a limitation on his freedom as much as it is an expression of his freedom.

19. Richard Bauckham provides an excellent and approachable discussion of God's relation to the dimensions of space and time in "The Incarnation and the Cosmic Christ," in *Incarnation: On the Scope and Depth of Christology*, ed. Niels Henrik Gregersen (Minneapolis: Fortress, 2015), 26–28.

20. Ibid.

21. The nature of the eternal God's exact relation to time is not without controversy even among those who might consider themselves classically orthodox. See Gregory Ganssle, ed., *God and Time: Four Views* (Downers Grove, IL: InterVarsity, 2001).

22. E.g., Millard Erickson lists holiness as an attribute of "the goodness of God" (*Christian Theology*, 256–58). While Erickson grants that God's holiness refers to his "uniqueness," he categorizes holiness as an attribute of "moral purity" (255–56).

23. As Kent E. Brower and Andy Johnson write in "Introduction: Holiness and the *Ekklēsia* of God," in *Holiness and Ecclesiology in the New Testament*, ed. Kent E. Brower and Andy Johnson (Grand Rapids: Eerdmans, 2007): "One thing that the OT, Second Temple Judaism, and the NT all agree on is that holiness is never an independent possession of an individual or a community. A community and people are holy only insofar as they are in relation to the Holy One" (xix). I will further argue in this book that apart from the Holy One himself, there is no thing, commodity, or property called "holiness." In regard to holiness, there is only God.

24. Leith, *Creeds of the Churches*, 33.

25. Ibid.

26. Ibid., 35.

27. Ibid., 36.

28. For an excellent and concise discussion of the doctrine of the hypostatic union, see Donald Macleod, *The Person of Christ* (Downers Grove, IL: InterVarsity, 1998), 188–93; cf. Bauckham, "Incarnation," 28–32. The question of the relation of the two natures of Jesus Christ was the primary concern of the Council of Chalcedon, which met in 451 in Chalcedon, which is today known as Kadikoy, a suburb of Istanbul, Turkey. For more on the Council of Chalcedon, especially as it relates to the question of Christology and the hypostatic union, see Justin S. Holcomb, *Know the Creeds and Councils* (Grand Rapids: Zondervan, 2014), 53–61; H. R. Macintosh, *The Doctrine of the Person of Jesus Christ* (Edinburgh: T&T Clark, 1937), 196–222; R. V. Sellers, *The Council of Chalcedon: A Historical and Doctrinal Survey* (London: SPCK, 1953); and Gerald Bray, *Creeds, Councils, and Christ* (Fearn: Mentor, 1997), 144–71.

29. According to Keith Warrington, *The Message of the Holy Spirit: The Spirit of Encounter* (Downers Grove, IL: InterVarsity Press, 2009), "When Luke records that Jesus returned in the power of the Spirit, he is referring to the fact that Jesus was functioning in the power of the Spirit." Warrington further notes that Luke's intention is to speak not primarily of the impact but of "the source of Jesus' power. . . . Jesus is functioning in nothing less than the power of the Spirit of God" (68).

30. This understanding of the Holy Spirit as the power for Christ's ministry and even his sinlessness has a long and significant history in Christian understanding. It may be found as early as Augustine and traced through Peter Lombard, John Calvin, the Westminster Confession, John Owen, and beyond. See Maarten Wisse and Hugo Meijer, "Pneumatology," in *A Companion to Reformed Orthodoxy*, ed. Herman J. Selderhuis (Leiden: Brill, 2013), 498–99; Gerald F. Hawthorne, *The Presence and the Power: The Significance of the Holy Spirit in the Life and Ministry of Jesus* (1991; repr., Eugene, OR: Wipf and Stock, 2003), 145–78.

31. Warrington, *Message of the Holy Spirit*, 68–69.

32. Webster, *Holiness*, 25.

33. Tony Clark, *Divine Revelation and Human Practice: Responsive and Imaginative Inspiration* (Eugene, OR: Cascade, 2008), 62, emphasis original. Cf. Beth Felker Jones, *Practicing Christian Doctrine: An Introduction to Thinking and Living Theologically* (Grand Rapids: Baker Academic, 2014), 31.

34. Webster, *Holiness*, 13.

35. According to Alister McGrath, *Christian Theology: An Introduction*, 5th ed. (Chichester: Blackwell, 2011), "The term 'apophatic' comes from the Greek word *apophatikos*, meaning 'negative,' which is derived from the verb 'to say no' or 'to deny.' It denotes an approach to theology which stresses that we cannot use human language to refer to God, who ultimately lies beyond such language. It is sometimes also referred to as the *via negativa* ('negative way')" (188). See also

Daniel Whistler, *Schelling's Theology of Symbolic Language: Forming the System of Identity* (New York: Oxford University Press, 2013), 221.

36. McGrath, *Christian Theology*, 188.

37. Ibid., 189–93.

38. This is true not only of what one may call "conservative" theology but also—and perhaps even more so—in other more "contemporary" theological traditions. As Gail Ramshaw writes in "The Gender of God," in *Feminist Theology: A Reader*, ed. Ann Loades (London: SPCK, 1990), "Theological language is to a great degree metaphoric. . . . We speak the metaphors with utter humility, believing in the God beyond the words and concluding our metaphoric speech to be so much straw" (170).

Chapter 4 Holiness and the Nature and Purpose of Humanity

1. Examples of this, even from a Christian perspective, are not difficult to find. They include John Ankerberg and John Weldon, *When Does Life Begin? And 39 Other Tough Questions about Abortion* (Brentwood, TN: Wolgemuth & Hyatt, 1989); and John L. Merritt and J. Lawrence Merritt, *When Does Human Life Begin? Scientific, Scriptural, and Historical Evidence Supports Implantation*, 3rd ed. (Kenmore, WA: Crystal Clear, 2012). In his presentation of the opinion of the US Supreme Court in the infamous *Roe v. Wade* case, Associate Justice Blackmun famously noted, "We need not resolve the difficult questions of when life begins. When those trained in the respective disciplines of medicine, philosophy, and theology are unable to arrive at any consensus, the judiciary, at this point in the development of man's knowledge, is not in a position to speculate as to the answer [of when life begins]." See Jerry D. Leonard, *Legal Studies as Cultural Studies: A Reader in (Post)Modern Critical Theory* (Albany: SUNY Press, 1995), 265.

2. For more on the relationship between ethical debates and various views of what it means to be human, see John Kilner, ed., *Why People Matter: A Christian Engagement with Rival Views of Human Significance* (Grand Rapids: Baker Academic, 2017).

3. Charles Darwin, *On the Origin of Species*, 5th ed. (New York: Appleton, 1871).

4. In *A Concise History of Modern Europe: Liberty, Equality, Solidarity*, 2nd ed. (Lanham: Rowman & Littlefield, 2011), David Mason writes, "An utter incompatibility existed between Darwin's theory of evolution and a literal interpretation of the Bible, particularly of the creation and Adam and Eve stories in Genesis. But the unpredictability of natural selection was also incompatible with the intelligent design argument of natural theology" (75). Mason goes on to describe how this incompatibility was worked out in Europe and North America.

5. These would, of course, include contemporary texts for whom Darwin is the direct target, such as Phillip E. Johnson, *Defeating Darwinism by Opening Minds* (Downers Grove, IL: InterVarsity, 1997); and Jonathan Wells, *The*

Politically Incorrect Guide to Darwinism and Intelligent Design (Washington, DC: Regnery, 2006).

6. Quoted in Bernard Weintraub, "Playboy Interview: Johnny Depp," *Playboy*, May 2004. The fact that Depp neither is seen as nor promotes himself as the paragon of holiness—and that this interview was conducted and published in a publication as profane as *Playboy*—only goes to show that the recognition of the breadth of human depravity is a concept that far outruns the confines of the church.

7. See, e.g., R. C. Sproul, *Chosen by God* (Wheaton: Tyndale, 1986), 80.

8. Such a position is clearly seen in the title of Cornelius Plantinga Jr.'s book on the theology of sin: *Not the Way It's Supposed to Be: A Breviary of Sin* (Grand Rapids: Eerdmans, 1996).

9. In *Church Dogmatics* III/2, *The Doctrine of Creation*, ed. G. W. Bromiley and T. F. Torrance, trans. G. W. Bromiley (Edinburgh: T&T Clark, 1960), Karl Barth describes the human condition in sin as humanity's denial of itself, "a mode of being contrary to [its] humanity" (197). Likewise, in *Incarnation: The Person and Life of Christ*, rev. ed. (Downers Grove, IL: InterVarsity, 2008), Thomas F. Torrance describes people in this situation as "less than human," "dehumanized," and "bastards and not true sons and daughters" (73).

10. Torrance writes:

> Here within our fallen and disobedient humanity, where we are less than human because of our sin, here where we have dehumanised ourselves in our rebellion, here where we, the sons and daughters of God, have become bastards and not true sons and daughters, he the Son of God become true Son of Man, true man for the first time in utter obedience, that is in true sonship toward God the Father. True man does not sin. True man is answering in truth the word of God addressed to mankind. Men and women who commit sin, who disobey the word of God, have fallen from their humanity into inhumanity. The commission of sin is no attribute of true humanity, but the attribute of inhumanity. But within this human-inhuman existence of Adam, Jesus Christ has come as the Son of God, the Son of Man as Jesus called himself, to live out a truly obedient and filial, that is, a truly human life, in perfect and unbroken communion with God the Father. (*Incarnation*, 73)

11. The three views I discuss here—substantive, functional, and relational—are treated at greater length in Erickson, *Christian Theology*, 462–69. Erickson notes that the idea that humans physically resemble God "has persisted even to this day," and he identifies the Church of Jesus Christ of Latter-day Saints (the Mormons) as holding to this view (461).

12. Erickson, *Christian Theology*, 465–67.

13. In asserting the dynamic nature of the image in this way, I am depending on but going beyond the view of those who would describe themselves as holding to the relational view but "propose that the image should be understood as the capacity for relations; in particular, it is the capacity for relationship with God," as Jason McMartin writes in "The Theandric Union as *Imago Dei* and *Capax*

Dei," in *Christology, Ancient and Modern*, ed. Oliver Crisp and Fred Sanders (Grand Rapids: Zondervan, 2013), 138.

14. In this distinction, which is not without its own challenges, I am referring to the work of twentieth-century Swiss theologian Emil Brunner. See Brunner, *Man in Revolt*, trans. Olive Wyon (London: Lutterworth, 1939), 91–98; Brunner, *The Christian Doctrine of Creation and Redemption*, trans. Olive Wyon (Philadelphia: Westminster, 1953), 55–56. See also Alister McGrath, *Emil Brunner: A Reappraisal* (Malden, MA: Wiley-Blackwell, 2014), 118–20, 145–48.

15. Brunner, *Man in Revolt*, 500–501; Erickson, *Christian Theology*, 463.

16. Brunner writes: "Figuratively speaking, God produces the other creatures in a finished state; they are what they ought to be, and this they remain. But God retains man within His workshop, within His hands. He does not simply make him and finish him; human nature, indeed, consists in the fact that we may and must remain the hands of God" (*Man in Revolt*, 97).

17. Ibid., 98.

18. This is one of the clear weaknesses of many of the manifestations of the various forms of what Millard Erickson has categorized as both the substantive and functional views. See Erickson, *Christian Theology*, 460–63, 465–67.

19. In *What the Bible Says about God the Creator* (1983; repr., Eugene, OR: Wipf and Stock, 2000), Jack Cottrell observes: "It is definitely true that God does not (indeed, cannot) share his kind of being with anything else. The fact of creation with the resulting Creator/creature distinction is an absolute barrier to any kind of shared being. The Creator's being and mode of being are of necessity different from that of all creatures. He alone is the Creator, existing in splendid majesty as uncreated being" (33). Richard Bauckham adds in *God Crucified* (Grand Rapids: Eerdmans, 1999) that the "answer given again and again . . . is that the only true God, YHWH, the God of Israel, is sole Creator of all things and sole Ruler of all things. . . . [Only] the God of Israel is worthy of worship because he is sole Creator of all things and sole Ruler of all things. Other beings who might otherwise be thought divine are by these criteria God's creatures and subjects" (10–11). Likewise, in *The Humanity of God*, trans. John Newton Thomas (Louisville: Westminster John Knox, 1960), Karl Barth describes God as "a God absolutely unique in His relation to man and the world, overpoweringly lofty and distant, strange, yes even wholly other" (37–38).

20. According to Vern S. Poythress, *Logic: A God-Centered Approach to the Foundation of Western Thought* (Wheaton: Crossway, 2013), "The Bible teaches that God the Creator is distinct from the creatures he has made. This distinction is called the *Creator-creature distinction*. There are two levels of being, God and creature, rather than one" (138, emphasis original).

21. In "Humanity—Created, Restored, Transformed, Embodied," in *Rethinking Human Nature: A Multidisciplinary Approach*, ed. Malcolm Jeeves (Grand Rapids: Eerdmans, 2011), Joel B. Green writes: "Humans are unlike other creatures in that only humanity is created after God's own likeness, in God's own image (imago dei). . . . Humanity thus stands in an ambivalent position—living

in solidarity with the rest of the created order and yet distant from it on account of humankind's unique role as the bearer of the divine image" (274).

22. It should be observed that this verse also describes humanity as created from the "dust of the ground," thereby connoting humanity's "creatureliness." See John H. Sailhamer, "Genesis," in *The Expositor's Bible Commentary* (Grand Rapids: Zondervan, 1990), 2:41.

23. John F. Kilner surveys the various historic positions regarding the degree to which the fall impacted the image in Kilner, *Dignity and Destiny: Humanity in the Image of God* (Grand Rapids: Eerdmans, 2015), 159–74.

24. "Although marred by sin, the image is still very much a reality," observes Donald W. Burdick in "James," in *The Expositor's Bible Commentary* (Grand Rapids: Zondervan, 1990), 12:188. See also Douglas J. Moo, *James* (Grand Rapids: Eerdmans, 1985), 128.

25. G. C. Berkouwer, *Man: The Image of God*, trans. Dirk W. Jellema (Grand Rapids: Eerdmans, 1962), 44.

26. In describing the nonessential character of sin in humanity, J. Todd Billings refers to the "accidental characteristic of sinning." See Billings, *Union with Christ: Reframing Theology and Ministry for the Church* (Grand Rapids: Baker Academic, 2011), 44.

27. As Walter Kasper writes in *Jesus the Christ*, new ed. (London: Continuum, 2011), "So Jesus Christ in person is the answer to the basic question of human existence and the key to understanding the meaning of all reality. In Jesus Christ, God both revealed himself and revealed humanity to human beings" (ix). Stanley J. Grenz likewise writes in *Theology for the Community of God* (Grand Rapids: Eerdmans, 2000) that the "declaration of Jesus' humanity means that he is the revelation of essential human nature, the exemplar of human fellowship or life-in-community" (304).

28. Hesketh Pearson, *George Bernard Shaw: His Life and Personality* (New York: Atheneum, 1963), 110.

29. As Grenz writes, "Having been created good, [Adam and Eve] were untainted by evil; they lived in innocency. Our first parents enjoyed fellowship with God, perhaps in that God regularly walked in the Garden in the cool of the day (Gen. 3:8). They savored community with each other, for they were naked and felt no shame (Gen. 2:25). And the first humans experienced harmony with the rest of creation" (*Theology for the Community of God*, 190–91).

30. *The Compact Edition of the Oxford English Dictionary*, vol. 2 (Oxford: Oxford University Press, 1971), s.v. "perfect."

31. Anselm, *Proslogion*, in *The Ontological Argument: From St. Anselm to Contemporary Philosophers*, ed. Alvin Plantinga (Garden City, NY: Anchor Books, 1965), 4.

32. *Confession of Faith*, 3.

33. "Our relationship with God is innate," writes Gerald Bray in *God Is Love: A Biblical and Systematic Theology* (Wheaton: Crossway, 2012), 308.

34. In *Ministry in the Image of God: The Trinitarian Shape of Christian Service* (Downers Grove, IL: InterVarsity, 2005), Stephen Seamands writes: "Of course, this participation doesn't mean . . . that our human nature actually becomes divine. God dwells in us and we dwell in God, but our radical divine-human differences are never blurred, nor do we ever merge with one another. Yet what a rich, joyous union with the triune God is offered to us" (12).

35. For an excellent source on the history and various expressions of the doctrine of divinization throughout church history, see Michael J. Christensen and Jeffery A. Wittung, eds., *Partakers of the Divine Nature: The History and Development of Deification in the Christian Traditions*, paperback ed. (Grand Rapids: Baker Academic, 2008).

36. As Ross Hastings writes in *Missional God, Missional Church* (Downers Grove, IL: IVP Academic, 2012), "It is relationality between human and divine persons that constitutes participation of humans in God, and in which human persons remain human and divine persons divine" (273).

Chapter 5 Holiness and the Nature and Problem of Sin

1. *Jaws*, directed by Steven Spielberg (Universal City, CA: Universal Pictures, 1975).

2. My presentation of these five terms follows Erickson, *Christian Theology*, 519–26.

3. R. Stanton Norman, "Human Sinfulness," in *A Theology for the Church*, ed. Daniel L. Akin (Nashville: B&H, 2007), 417; Erickson, *Christian Theology*, 519.

4. Norman, "Human Sinfulness," 417.

5. As Norman describes, "The moral connotations of the concept stipulate that a person misses the right mark because he intentionally chooses to aim at a wrong mark; he misses the right path because he deliberately chooses to follow a wrong path. . . . With regard to moral culpability, there is no question of an innocent mistake or a negative idea of failure. The term suggests an active, deliberate missing of the right mark or way in order to choose intentionally a wrong mark or path. The sinner is responsible and accountable for the behavior that results in missing the mark, whether overtly intentional or not" ("Human Sinfulness," 418). For more on the idea of the intentionality of sin contained in this metaphor for sin, see Derek Johnston, *A Brief History of Theology: From the New Testament to Feminist Theology* (London: Continuum, 2008), 43; Michael Bird, *Evangelical Theology: A Biblical and Systematic Introduction* (Grand Rapids: Zondervan, 2013), 668.

6. Norman, "Human Sinfulness," 415; Erickson, *Christian Theology*, 521.

7. Robert Yarbrough, "Sin in the Gospels, Acts, and Hebrews to Revelation," in *Fallen: A Theology of Sin*, ed. Christopher W. Morgan and Robert A. Peterson (Wheaton: Crossway, 2013), 102–5; Erickson, *Christian Theology*, 521.

8. Yarbrough explains, "The word can denote not just a falling short of God's moral law (like 'sin' often does) but a positive and extreme rejection of that law" ("Sin in the Gospels," 100). Cf. Erickson, *Christian Theology*, 522.

9. Walter Brueggemann, *Interpretation and Obedience: From Faithful Reading to Faithful Living* (Minneapolis: Fortress, 1991), 294; Erickson, *Christian Theology*, 522.

10. Ergun Caner, "Sin," in *The Popular Encyclopedia of Apologetics: Surveying the Evidence for the Truth of Christianity*, ed. Ed Hindson and Ergun Caner (Eugene, OR: Harvest House, 2008), 452.

11. Donald Fairbairn, *Life in the Trinity: An Introduction to Theology with the Help of the Church Fathers* (Downers Grove, IL: IVP Academic, 2009), 99.

12. Erickson, *Christian Theology*, 523.

13. Fairbairn, *Life in the Trinity*, 99.

14. D. K. McKim, "Disobedience," in *The International Standard Bible Encyclopedia*, rev. ed., gen. ed. Geoffrey W. Bromiley (Grand Rapids: Eerdmans, 1979), 1:961; Erickson, *Christian Theology*, 523–24.

15. According to Ben Witherington III, *The Problem with Evangelical Theology: Testing the Exegetical Foundations of Calvinism, Dispensationalism, and Wesleyanism* (Waco: Baylor University Press, 2005), *paraptōma*, a Greek word related to *parapiptō* also used in the New Testament to describe sin, "has a narrow range of meaning and seems in fact to refer to willful violations of known laws or principles or objective standards" (210). While the meaning that Witherington provides here may press the categorization of "treachery," it nevertheless still rests well within the category of "rebellion." See also Erickson, *Christian Theology*, 525.

16. As William Barclay describes in *The Apostles' Creed* (Louisville: Westminster John Knox, 1998), the "basic idea of [this word] is distortion or perversion. It thinks of sin as that which distorts and perverts what is right" (256). See also Danielle Celermajer, *The Sins of the Nation and the Ritual of Apologies* (New York: Cambridge University Press, 2009), 91; David Birnbaum and Benjamin Blech, *Sanctification* (New York: New Paradigm Matrix, 2014), 387.

17. John Reumann, *Philippians: A New Translation with Introduction and Commentary*, The Anchor Yale Bible Commentaries (New Haven: Yale University Press, 2008), 392.

18. Nora J. Opperwall, "Crooked," in *International Standard Bible Encyclopedia*, 1:825.

19. Timothy Patrick Jackson, *Love Disconsoled: Meditations on Christian Charity* (New York: Cambridge University Press, 1999), 99. Jackson cites New Testament scholar Leon Morris, who notes that there are four such words. Two, however, are formal differences derived from a common root. See Leon L. Morris, "Abomination," in *The New Bible Dictionary*, ed. J. D. Douglas (Grand Rapids: Eerdmans, 1967), 4. Cf. M. H. Lovelace, "Abomination," in *The Interpreters Dictionary of the Bible*, ed. G. A. Buttrick (Nashville: Abingdon, 1962), 1:12–13; Erickson, *Christian Theology*, 526.

20. J. Reiling and J. L. Swellengrebel, *A Translator's Handbook on the Gospel of Luke* (Leiden: Brill, 1971), 567; Jackson, *Love Disconsoled*, 99.

21. Erickson, *Christian Theology*, 526. Erickson offers a list of such practices, including idolatry, child sacrifice, and witchcraft.

22. As Jonathan R. Wilson writes in *A Primer for Christian Doctrine* (Grand Rapids: Eerdmans, 2005), "One of the primary ways of developing a doctrine of sin is by viewing it as a relational concept" (91).

23. According to Wilson, "In relationship to God, sin(s) may be regarded as disobedience to God. Or sin(s) may also be viewed as breaking other relationships for which we are created, such as our relationship to one another, to the rest of creation, and to ourselves" (*Primer for Christian Doctrine*, 91).

24. José Morales provides a thoughtful and provocative discussion on this idea in a chapter titled "Man's Dominion of Nature" in Morales, *Creation Theology*, trans. Michael Adams and Dudley Cleary (Dublin: Four Courts, 2001), 238–50.

25. As Ben Witherington III writes in *The Indelible Image: The Theological and Ethical Thought World of the New Testament*, vol. 2, *The Collective Witness* (Downers Grove, IL: IVP Academic, 2010), "Sin was always a sin against God and so was inherently a theological problem. . . . [Sin] was seen as an affront to a holy God, and assault on God's principle and place, a rejection of God's rule, a corruption of God's image in humankind—in short, an intolerable violation of God's character by the image of God" (74). For a more focused treatment of "sin as offense against God's honor," see Derek R. Nelson, *Sin: A Guide for the Perplexed* (London: T&T Clark, 2011), 9–16.

26. New Testament scholar Douglas Moo notes in "The Law of Christ as the Fulfillment of the Law of Moses: A Modified Lutheran View," in *Five Views on Law and Gospel*, ed. Greg L. Bahnsen et al. (Grand Rapids: Zondervan, 1996), that the law "was God's gracious revelation of this character, and it demanded that those who were now his people become like him in character." He goes on to say, "God's character is the implied basis for the entire law; in different ways, its various commandments and prohibitions spell out implications of his character for his people Israel" (335).

27. In their book *Unshakable Foundations: Contemporary Answers to Crucial Questions about the Christian Faith* (Bloomington, MN: Bethany House, 2001), Norman L. Geisler and Peter Bocchino write that since "the moral law is based upon the nature of God, any violation of that law is in reality a violation against God alone (Ps. 51:4a). This includes all sins—even sins against ourselves—because we are created in God's image, and all that is good in us is a reflection of the image of God. When we devalue ourselves or devalue others, it is equivalent to devaluing the true image of God in us and in them. So whether we deface (sin against) the image of God in us or in someone else, we ultimately sin against God" (365).

28. *Random House Unabridged Dictionary* (2006), s.v. "political correctness."

29. *Random House Unabridged Dictionary* (2006), s.v. "tolerance."

30. James I. Packer, *Rediscovering Holiness* (Ann Arbor, MI: Vine, 1992), 68.

31. Karl Menninger, *Whatever Became of Sin?* (New York: Hawthorne, 1973), 14.

Chapter 6 Holiness and the Nature and Goal of Salvation

1. Though not all may agree with my definition of foreknowledge, the link between it and holiness, scripturally speaking, remains beyond reasonable dispute.

For a concise survey of various positions on the doctrine of foreknowledge, see John S. Feinberg, *The Many Faces of Evil: Theological Systems and the Problems of Evil*, rev. ed. (Wheaton: Crossway, 2004), 107–18. See also James K. Beilby and Paul R. Eddy, eds., *Divine Foreknowledge: Four Views* (Downers Grove, IL: InterVarsity, 2001).

2. So, e.g., Paul writes to the Colossians: "When you were dead in your sins and in the uncircumcision of your flesh, God made you alive with Christ. He forgave us all our sins" (Col. 2:13; cf. Eph. 2:1).

3. Cf. the similar pattern in John 5:24.

4. The idea of *ransom* is related to that of redemption. Ransom was one of Jesus's own metaphors for his work: "For even the Son of Man did not come to be served, but to serve, and to give his life as a ransom for many" (Mark 10:45; see also 1 Tim. 2:5–6). Jesus's words note that humanity's redemption has come at both a great and deeply personal cost to the redeemer.

5. This metaphor seems to be a particular favorite of Paul's and, beyond his letter to the Romans, is found in 1 Cor. 6:11; Gal. 2:16–17; 3:24; Phil. 3:9; and Titus 3:7, just to name a few. In addition to Paul's writings, it is also found in James 2, though historically some (most notably sixteenth-century Reformer Martin Luther) have argued that James's message regarding the meaning of justification is distinct from Paul's.

6. Cf. Ps. 7:11; 2 Tim. 4:8.

7. "For in the gospel the righteousness of God is revealed—a righteousness that is by faith from first to last, just as it is written: 'The righteous will live by faith.'"

8. As Luther states: "Thus a Christian man is righteous and a sinner at the same time, holy and profane, an enemy of God and a child of God." See Martin Luther, *Lectures on Galatians* (1535), in *Luther's Works*, American Edition, ed. Jaroslav Pelikan and Helmut T. Lehmann (St. Louis: Concordia, 1955–86), 26:232.

9. Ibid., 106. Luther, however, was not alone. John Calvin (1509–1564), the great Reformer from Geneva, also noted that the doctrine of justification by grace alone, through faith alone, in Christ alone, is "the main hinge on which religion turns, so that we 'devote the greater attention and care to it.'" See John Calvin, *Institutes of the Christian Religion*, ed. John T. McNeill, trans. Ford Lewis Battles (Philadelphia: Westminster, 1960), 3.11.2.

10. Luther, *Lectures on Galatians* (1535), in *Luther's Works*, 26:9.

11. Luther, *Lectures on the Psalms of Ascent and Psalm 90* (1532/1535), in *Martin Luthers Werke*, Kritische Gesamtausgabe (Weimar, Germany: Böhlau, 1930), 40/3:352.

12. Luther, *Lectures on Galatians* (1535), in *Luther's Works*, 27:9.

13. For some, such a view is the natural consequence of Luther's doctrine of justification, the complete obliteration of any place for works (or of holiness) in the Christian life, at least in the present age. Just one example is seen in the theology and practice of Luther's own student Johann Agricola (1494–1566). Agricola took Luther's dogged emphasis on and commitment to justification by grace and its corollary (not by works) and concluded that since works do not produce salvation

and since the central teaching of the Christian faith is that of grace, works play no role in the Christian life whatsoever. In spite of what we might think about the natural consequences of Luther's theology, he vehemently opposed the teaching of Agricola. Luther, it is said, coined the term "antinomianism," which literally means "against or contrary to the law," to refer to this teaching. See R. D. Linder, "Antinomianism," in *Evangelical Dictionary of Theology*, ed. Walter A. Elwell, 2nd ed. (Grand Rapids: Baker Academic, 2001), 70–72. In spite of Luther's disavowals of this view as a legitimate interpretation of his theology, the history of antinomianism within the Protestant tradition is long and storied. See Mark Jones, *Antinomianism: Reformed Theology's Unwelcome Guest?* (Phillipsburg, NJ: P&R, 2013), 1–18. To this day, Luther's theological progeny remain susceptible to Agricola's error. Even within evangelicalism, there are those who would assert that justification in particular and God's saving work in general are divorced from human activity in any way, such that human activity neither contributes to nor necessarily results from justification. This would include those I refer to in this chapter's excursus as people who exercise "license."

14. Of particular note here is the work of the Finnish Lutheran theologian Tuomo Mannermaa, who argues that Luther's doctrine of justification is far more ontological and mystical than it has been portrayed to be. See Mannermaa, *Christ Present in Faith: Luther's View of Justification* (Minneapolis: Fortress, 2005); Carl E. Braaten and Robert W. Jenson, eds., *Union with Christ: The New Finnish Interpretation of Luther* (Grand Rapids: Eerdmans, 1998).

15. "Metaphoric myopia" is a term I use to describe what happens whenever one becomes so enamored with the power of a single metaphor to shed light on a given theological mystery that one fails to recognize the equally valid and perhaps necessary contributions of other biblical metaphors that address the very same mystery. The term is also used in economics to describe a similar phenomenon. See, e.g., Charles Wankel and Agata Stachowicz-Stanusch, *Handbook of Research on Teaching Ethics in Business and Management Education* (Hershey, PA: Information Science Reference, 2012).

16. So convinced was Luther of his own interpretation of the centrality of justification that he cast more than a shadow on the entire Epistle of James and its perceived emphasis on the role of works. He famously wrote, "Therefore, St. James's epistle is really an epistle of straw, compared to these others [the epistles of Paul and the remaining epistles of the New Testament], for it has nothing of the nature of the gospel about it." See Martin Luther, "Preface to the New Testament, 1546 (1522)," in *Word and Sacrament I*, in *Luther's Works*, 35:362.

17. Stephen Gabriel Rosenberg, *The Haphtara Cycle* (Northvale, NJ: Aronson, 2000), 4.

18. N. T. Wright, "New Perspectives on Paul," in *Justification in Perspective: Historical Developments and Contemporary Challenges*, ed. Bruce L. McCormack (Grand Rapids: Baker Academic, 2006), 251–52; Peter Toon, *Justification and Sanctification* (Westchester, IL: Crossway, 1983), 14.

19. Toon, *Justification and Sanctification*, 14.

20. Ibid., 24.

21. We should be sure to note that in his description of the "new creation" Paul communicates that humanity will result not only in a new kind of being (an ontological change) but, as denoted in Eph. 2:10, in a particular kind of behavior (a moral change).

22. This view of the goal of salvation is not exclusive to a particular arm of Protestant evangelicalism. It is found in both the Wesleyan-Arminian wing and the Reformed camp. Thus in his sermon "On Perfection," §76, in *First Series of Sermons (40–53) and Second Series Begun (54–86)*, vol. 6 of *The Works of John Wesley*, 3rd ed. (Kansas City, MO: Beacon Hill, 1978), John Wesley writes that Paul "leaves us no room to doubt, but God will thus 'renew us in the spirit of our mind' and 'create us anew' in the image of God, wherein we were first created" (416). And Reformed theologian Anthony A. Hoekema, summing up the argument he has been proposing for pages earlier in *Created in God's Image* (Grand Rapids: Eerdmans, 1986), suggests much the same thing: "Here again we see that the purpose of redemption is to restore the image of God in man" (27).

23. Genesis 9:6 directly links humanity's creation in the image of God with the prohibition to murder. It seems likely that the prohibition is not based solely on the manner in which or the form by which humanity was originally created but is based in part on that image continuing to reside at least to some degree within humanity.

24. One might fairly say that all the other effects of sin are merely manifestations of the damage done to the image.

25. This idea is central to Athanasius's argument in his highly influential text, *De Incarnatione*. See Athanasius, *St. Athanasius on the Incarnation: The Treatise "De Incarnatione Verbi Dei,"* trans. and ed. by a religious of CSMV (Crestwood, NY: St. Vladimir's Seminary Press, 1953).

26. Undoubtedly, this phrase "to be like God" would remind Paul's readers of the Genesis account of the creation of humanity, where God created humanity "in our likeness" (Gen. 1:26). It may also evoke within his hearers a memory of Gen. 3:5, where the serpent tells Eve, "For God knows that when you eat from it your eyes will be opened, and you will be like God, knowing good and evil." The key difference, however, is that in Paul's usage the change in nature is the result of God's gracious activity and not of humanity's usurping of his authority.

27. On this point Bridges writes, "If we have experienced [God's grace] at all, we will experience not only forgiveness of our sins but also freedom from sin's dominion" (*Pursuit of Holiness*, 34).

28. As Alexander writes, "The biblical doctrine of salvation also contains the promise of freedom from the tyranny of sin's control and the capacity to walk in righteousness and holiness" (*Pursuit of Godliness*, 6).

29. Ibid., 37. Alexander describes the *imago dei* minimally as the ability to understand and respond to God's command: "Created in God's image means that the human creature possesses those distinct qualities or characteristics (self-reflective reason, free-will, moral awareness, self-consciousness, self-determination, creativity,

etc.) which identifies the human to be like God" and which enables, though does not ensure, that it may freely follow God (ibid.).

30. As Barth writes, "It is never freedom to sin" (*Church Dogmatics* III/2, 197).

31. Helmut Thielicke, *The Freedom of the Christian Man: A Christian Confrontation with the Secular Gods*, trans. John W. Doberstein (New York: Harper & Row, 1963), 22.

32. As Paul Legarde writes, "He is not free who can do what he wills, but rather he who can become what he should" (cited in Thielicke, *Freedom of the Christian Man*, 10).

33. True freedom, according to Hoekema, is "the ability of humans, with the help of the Holy Spirit, to think, say, and do what is pleasing to God in harmony with his revealed will" (*Created in God's Image*, 228). See also Barth, *Church Dogmatics* III/2, 194–202.

34. Hoekema, *Created in God's Image*, 243. Ironically, Scripture describes even this relationship with God as enslavement: "But now that you have been set free from sin and have become slaves of God, the benefit you reap leads to holiness, and the result is eternal life" (Rom. 6:22).

Chapter 7 Holiness and the Nature and Goal of the Church

1. Ignatius of Antioch, "To the Smyrneans," in *The Apostolic Fathers*, 3rd ed., ed. and trans. Michael W. Holmes (Grand Rapids: Baker, 2007), 249. For more on the church fathers' writings on the church as "holy," see Angelo Di Berardino, ed., *We Believe in One Holy Catholic and Apostolic Church* (Downers Grove, IL: IVP Academic, 2010), 69–72.

2. The Canadian Indian residential school system was a "government-funded, church-run" network of boarding schools where Canadian aboriginal children were sent not only to be educated but also, just as important, to be assimilated into Canadian (that is, Caucasian) culture. In addition to the explicit mandate of cultural genocide—to "kill the Indian in the child"—the incidents of physical and sexual abuse that occurred at these schools, including rape and forced sterilization, are myriad. For more information, see Truth and Reconciliation Commission of Canada, *Honouring the Truth, Reconciling for the Future: Summary of the Final Report of the Truth and Reconciliation Commission of Canada* (Toronto: Createspace, 2015).

3. Thomas C. Oden, *Systematic Theology*, vol. 3, *Life in the Spirit* (San Francisco: HarperCollins, 1992), 316.

4. Edmund P. Clowney, *The Church* (Downers Grove, IL: InterVaristy, 1995), 84.

5. Brad Harper and Paul Louis Metzger, *Exploring Ecclesiology: An Evangelical and Ecumenical Introduction* (Grand Rapids: Brazos, 2009), 19.

6. This covenant is reiterated directly and indirectly in other places in the Old Testament, particularly in Jeremiah (7:23; 11:4; 30:22) and Ezekiel (36:28).

7. *Confession of Faith*, 3.

8. As David G. Peterson writes in *Possessed by God: A New Testament Theology of Sanctification and Holiness* (Downers Grove, IL: IVP Academic, 2001), "In the

final analysis, Israel's task as a 'holy nation' was to sanctify the Lord before the nations by responding appropriately to him as the Holy One" (24).

9. For more on the interpretation of the phrase *extra ecclesiam nulla salus*, see Veli-Matti Kärkkäinen, *An Introduction the Theology of Religions: Biblical, Historical, and Contemporary Perspectives* (Downers Grove, IL: IVP Academic, 2003), 78–81.

10. Webster, *Holiness*, 80.

11. Craig Van Gelder, *The Essence of the Church: A Community Created by the Spirit* (Grand Rapids: Baker Books, 2000), 108.

12. Colin E. Gunton, *The Christian Faith: An Introduction to Christian Doctrine* (Oxford: Blackwell, 2002), 128.

13. Clowney, *Church*, 88.

14. Van Gelder, *Essence of the Church*, 116.

15. As Anthony C. Thiselton writes in *The First Epistle to the Corinthians: A Commentary on the Greek Text* (Grand Rapids: Eerdmans, 2000), "God's presence *constitutes* the temple status of his people, and without it they are no temple" (317, emphasis original). Likewise, Menahem Haran writes in *Temples and Temple-Service in Ancient Israel* (1978; repr., Winona Lake, IN: Eisenbrauns, 1985), "By its very nature, a temple was considered to be a divine dwelling" (16). See also Tremper Longman III, *Immanuel in Our Place: Seeing Christ in Israel's Worship* (Phillipsburg, NJ: P&R, 2001), 32, 47; D. Stephen Long, *Hebrews* (Louisville: Westminster John Knox, 2011), 157; and Yves M.-J. Congar, *The Mystery of the Temple, Or, The Manner of God's Presence to His Creatures from Genesis to the Apocalypse*, trans. Reginald F. Trevett (Westminster, MD: Newman, 1962).

16. In 1 Thess. 4, Paul talks about how the Thessalonians are "to live in order to please God" and to do so "more and more" (4:1). Paul instructs them on some of the ways they are to do so: "you should avoid sexual immorality . . . [and] learn to control your own body in a way that is holy and honorable, not in passionate lust like the pagans, who do not know God" (4:3–5).

17. Calvin, *Institutes*, 4.1.17.

18. While the idea of confession is often associated with verbal proclamation, the church's confession is always to be in both word and deed. Indeed, not only is the church's confession grounded in its holiness, but its practice of holiness is a key form of its confession. See, e.g., Morna D. Hooker, "Be Holy as I Am Holy," in Morna D. Hooker and Frances Young, *Holiness and Mission: Learning from the Early Church about Mission in the City* (London: SCM, 2010), 4–18.

19. In order to understand Donatism, one must first become acquainted with the nature of Christian persecution under Roman emperor Diocletian (245–313). Beginning in 303, Diocletian, who considered himself a demi-god, issued a series of edicts demanding the empire-wide revival of traditional Roman religious practices and denying the legal and civil rights of the emerging Christian church. Two of these edicts are of particular note. The first outlawed Christianity, called for the destruction of church buildings, and required the surrender and subsequent burning of its sacred texts. The fourth edict, issued the very next year, demanded that

everyone offer sacrifice to the traditional Roman deities. Failure to comply with these edicts left one subject to death. Perhaps because of his distance from Rome, the Roman governor of North Africa was often satisfied just to receive copies of Scripture from church leaders, taking such submission as a practical repudiation of their Christian faith. Not all Christian leaders, however, were willing to give in even to these lesser demands. Consequently, some were mistreated and some were martyred. Those who did succumb to the pressure of the Roman edicts by surrendering their copies of the Scriptures to local authorities were derogatorily branded *traditores*, the Latin term for "those who hand things over."

Understandably, many were disappointed in the *traditores*. The most fervently opposed to the *traditores* were the Donatists. The Donatists noted that an early church Father, Tertullian (155–240), denied that Christians were allowed to flee persecution. In the eyes of the Donatists, then, all traditores had abandoned the faith by surrendering the Scriptures to worldly authorities in order to be spared persecution or death.

For more on Donatism, see W. H. C. Frend, *The Donatist Church: A Movement of Protest in Roman North Africa* (Oxford: Clarendon, 1971); Ben Quash, "Donatism: Do Christian Ministers Need to Be Faultless for Their Ministrations to Be Effective?" in Quash and Ward, *Heresies and How to Avoid Them*, 81–90.

Conclusion

1. Reginald Heber, "Holy, Holy, Holy," in *Hymns of the Christian Life*, 2.

Index